Dedicated to my five wonderful children, Evan, Brianna, Kayla, Zachary, and Rachel, who always believe in me, and my loving husband Dale, without whose support this book may never have been written. Also to my mother, Linda, for encouraging me from childhood.

Note: Please use good judgement when determining whether a project or idea in this book is appropriate for your situation. The author does not take responsibility for results of any decorating project, and urges you always to keep safety a priority in your home, especially where children are concerned.

Table Of Contents:

Chapter Eight
Favorite Projects

Chapter Nine

Chapter One

Introduction To Creative Budget Decorating

Welcome to Quick Decorating Ideas, I know you will find it packed full of creative ideas and inspiration to enhance your home, all for less than $20! I want to offer you a few general decorating tips before you get started. I hope once you've finished this introduction you'll be ready to take your home room by room, and apply some of the ideas you'll gather from reading this book. My goal is to help you transform your home into a personal, warm, inviting place, even with the tightest budget.

You can do it without spending large amounts of money, money we could all use elsewhere!

Utilize note taking to jot down ideas you have, color combinations you love, or problems you need to solve. Keep track of your theme ideas or write down an idea you get from a decorating show or magazine. Make note of something from the book that sparks an idea, or reveals a problem. Make a divided notebook with a different section for each room, and review it often.

Use the ideas in this book to spark your own imagination, and don't stop here! Always keep your eyes and your mind open for "budget" opportunities.

Though I don't believe in rules when it comes to decorating *your* space, here are some guidelines to help you get started.

1. Trust yourself. This is my most important piece of advice. You know a lot more about what works than you think- if it looks great to your eye, that's all that really matters, its YOUR HOME!

2. Select the most important object in the room, and make it your focal point. For instance, the fireplace in a room makes a classic focal point, and furnishings and objects are arranged around it. There can be and often is more than one focal point, but they are secondary to the main one. Also, if you spend your money on one nice quality item in the room, then the budget ideas that support it are all the more convincing.

1

3. Set a theme for each room. (See "Theme Ideas" in this first chapter for inspiration). It helps tremendously! You wouldn't write a story without a main idea, would you?
   Even if your theme is just a color combo that you love, it will give you a starting point and guide you.
4. Work from the largest part of a room to the smallest when planning your design. For instance, start with walls, then windows, floors, furnishings, and accessories. The larger the decorating surface, the more impact it will have.
5. A word about combining color and pattern. The easiest way to pick color combos that work is to borrow from a piece of fabric or wall covering to be used in that room.

For instance, take a floral fabric to be used on seat cushions.

Choose one color from the fabric for the walls, one for the curtains and pillows, one or two for the accessories…you get the idea. Or use those magazine photos, and borrow one of your favorite color schemes. Some great web sites to peruse for ideas- www.bhg.com, www.countryliving.com, www.housebeautiful.com, or visit our resource section in the back of this book.

You can combine pattern- choose one dominant pattern, then use several different less dominant patterns, with at least one shared color in each one. "Less dominant" refers to a pattern smaller in scale, or subtler in color than the dominant pattern. Use each pattern in at least two places in the room and try not to get too crazy, unless that's the look you are after! I find that using no more than five different patterns in a room keep it from being too busy.

6. Have fun! Part of the satisfaction in decorating your home yourself is being proud of your creativity! We are ALL creative. Use these ideas to find it in yourself.

Other than that, there are no real rules except for the ones you set for yourself.

Organize for Creativity

OK, well, I know organization isn't really decorating, now is it? But, let's face it; what good is all the effort to create a nice home when it's hidden behind the mess and the clutter? So in order to help us all prevail over the chaos, here are some great hints for putting everything in its place! (On a budget, of course!)

The number one way to reduce clutter and mess? Deal with things as they occur, don't save it for later. File the mail (or throw it away) as soon as it comes out of the mailbox. Don't step over a small mess thinking you'll do the whole room later. Get the idea? File your paperwork. Make a file/correspondence box with file folders. I just covered a sturdy cardboard box with some contact paper, turned it on its side, and glued a piece of miniature picket fence (cut out of leftover foam core) onto the front to hold in the bills. You could save lightweight cardboard for dividers, make a "to pay" file and a "to keep" file, and perhaps a school file for the kids, and whatever else fits your household!

Hide stuff! Yes, there are times when we don't want our living room to look like Disneyland. Floor length cloths over the end tables is a great place to shove a toy box or unusually shaped toys when not needed. If you have open shelving or a pantry area, consider sewing a gathered curtain panel to cover clutter. Install it with a spring-tension curtain rod, tie it on with ribbon, or try my favorite, velcro stick-on tabs!

Organize your kitchen logically, and not only will you reduce clutter, you'll save time and energy! Place items in cupboards near the area where you normally use them.

For instance, spices near the stove, everyday dishes near the dishwasher, cutting board and knives near the sink - you get the idea! Use small boxes turned upside-down to make higher "shelves" in the back of your spice cabinet.

You don't have to buy expensive storage cubes for your kids' rooms. Covered boxes, sewn drawstring bags from extra material, even an old suitcase under the bed make good storage. A wall of simple metal-strip utility shelving (they sell it in white, as well) can accommodate a large amount of stuff, especially for the older kids, and is relatively cheap at home improvement stores. I save old baby-wipe containers to store crayons, hot wheels, and that endless supply of useless toys from the fast food joints! You can cover them with contact paper. Try labeling what goes where, even for the older kids, so there is no arguing about what "putting it away" really means!

Finally, attack one area at a time. Try to fit in a little re-organizing each day, and you'll be recognizing that creative décor you lost in the clutter again soon!

Redesigning Your Rooms (Without needing a moving man!)

There is a simple technique to rearranging your rooms, even over and over if you need to. Simply get yourself some graph paper, (you can print it off many computer programs) and measure your room. Using a scale of one square=one foot (or whatever scale works for you, just be sure to write it down and use it consistently) mark out the dimensions of your room, being sure to include placement of doors, windows, and walkthroughs, and also anything else important such as cable or phone outlets.

Now, measure your furniture length and depth. Using the same graph paper and scale, cut out representations of all the furniture you will, or could use in that room. For example, using 1 square=1 foot scale…my couch is 7 feet long, and 3 feet deep. The template piece representing my couch would be 7 squares long, by 3 squares deep. It helps to color the templates before cutting them out to make them more visible against the white paper background.

Now simply place the templates on the room drawing, and rearrange to your hearts content! This is a great way to try out new ideas for furniture placement, it will prevent you from moving that couch into that corner, only to find out it doesn't fit, or you hadn't thought it would cover that much of the window, and then having to move it back! It also allows you to be more creative in your thinking since all you're doing is pushing paper, until you find the perfect arrangement for your room!

Creative Sources for Materials

Use your imagination when looking for sources of material for your decorating and crafting projects. For instance, fabric is found in a lot more places than just the sewing store!

How about a favorite old sweater recycled into a throw pillow cover? Or the seat of a pair of worn-out jeans for a pillow on a child's bed or chair? An old striped button down shirt could recover that extra chair in the corner, or that beautiful old skirt, stained on one side, could make accessories for the family room.

Thrift stores and garage sales are great places to find usable material for next to nothing, and the bigger the size, (for once) the better! (More material!)

Old worn out blankets make great linings for quilts, potholders, quilted curtains and shades, etc....

Tablecloths and cloth napkins, either your own or purchased at yard sales, make wonderful material for projects, or can be made into window treatments and throw pillows with little or no sewing.

Cardboard cereal boxes make excellent bases for fabric covered picture frames. Many "snap on lid" type containers can be dressed up and used for desk top storage, small toy pieces, tea bags, etc....

Large corrugated boxes, or TV and stereo boxes still packed with their Styrofoam, make great end tables when covered with fabric. This way, you don't have to store empty boxes, and your husband can sleep well at night knowing that he will always have the appropriate packing for the treasured TV!

Boxes can also be covered and used to add height to a tabletop or cabinet display. If they have a removable lid, they can be covered and stacked for storage, similar to hatboxes.

Sheets are a great value, especially if you watch for good sales. Twin-size flats seem to be the best value, and are easier to work with. If you find a great sale, but don't have a project in mind, pick up white ones. You can always dye them, or stamp/stencil them later to meet your needs.

Free houseplants? Take ivy cuttings from outdoors, root in water, then pot up! You could even ask a neighbor for permission to take cuttings if you don't have any in your yard. Shade annuals bought on sale also make beautiful, cheap flowering houseplants. Impatiens, begonias, primroses, and pansies in six packs are great values as they grow quickly.

Look at things in new ways, and learn to see things for what they "could" be, instead of what they are!

Theme Ideas

Here are some ideas to get you started picking out a theme for your room. This is by no means a conclusive list; please use it as a jumping off point. If you don't see something here that you like, let your creativity spark an idea near and dear to you to make your rooms as personal as possible.

Look through all your favorite magazines, and don't be afraid to steal an idea you really love. Remember, a theme can even be as simple as a color or pattern combination.

Or, try these.

Nature themes are really big now. I think it must have something to do with desiring a simpler, more grounded existence in this busy world, but whatever the reason, it's a great theme, one that I use in my own house. It can be as simple as your favorite flower, fruit, or animal.

An all over organic look, a jungle, tropical theme. The woodsy lodge look can fit into this category, as well as the southwest look. Use lots of nature inspired materials and accessories...wood, grass cloth, sisal, stone. (Remember those cheap faux paint finishes!) Botanical prints, leaf patterns, dried material wreaths. Take long walks in the woods, fields, and beaches for collected items that can be used.

European country themes. For most of us, these tend to blend together, and that's just fine. The most important identifier of this theme is the fabric and colors you choose for your rooms. This is a time when those magazines come in handy!

American country. This is a theme where a crafter or sewer can be in heaven! Handmade items are key, with old-fashioned fabrics such as gingham and lace and calico. Quilts, hearts, antiques, and family treasures are important here. By the way, all antiques are NOT expensive, but more on that later.

Theme your room around a favorite past time...my husband is very into motorcycles, so I designed his bathroom with his favorite memorabilia, everything from tee shirts on the walls, to baseball hats, to framed certificates. The same could be done for a bowler, fisherman, sports lover, racing fan, or gardener, sailor, photographer, writer, skier, etc...

Again, all this is just a jumping off point. Remember, the idea is to develop a theme personal to you and your family.

Use What You Have!

The best budget strategy!

Decorating with what you have has become a very popular concept, and with good reason. Budget decorators more than anyone else can benefit from looking at things they already own, in a new way. What's better than free? Here are some great ideas for using your own things, and making your rooms look new again!

Look through your drawers for items of clothing that may be useful. A pretty shawl in the right color scheme may be just what you need to drape over that tired sofa, or how about draped over your mantel? Old clothing can often be fashioned into pillow covers, picture frame covers, chair seats, etc... Our clothing usually represents our tastes in color and texture; you may be surprised at how much from your closet fits into your room scheme. Reuse it as fabric in your projects!

Look for unused containers for unusual plant arrangements.

Old teapots, steins, pitchers, and gravy boats can make a charming vignette when filled with greenery. Those same old teapots can make great accessories, too.

Scour your linen closet for lace, cloth napkins, pretty tablecloths that are too special for everyday use, and think of how you may be able to use them differently in the home. Lace can be used in so many ways! Try softening shelf edges with doilies, or folded napkins. Twist and drape a tablecloth or sheet over a curtain rod for a fresh new window covering. Slip throw pillows into embroidered pillowcases, and tie closed with a silky cord for a romantic touch. Use placemats over a curtain rod as a valance. Use your imagination!

7

Search your basement for old furniture that has been outdated, and see if you can make it into something wonderful! Painted finishes are very in now, so it is possible to make that 1970's bookcase into a beautiful china display case. Or that peeling wooden chair into great extra seating, or if it isn't sturdy, how about a great artistic plant stand for the foyer?

Check your garden for ornaments that can be brought in the home. How about a rustic birdbath filled with dried flowers in an entry, or garden tools hung on the wall, or in a bucket on a shelf? Large pots can be made into end, sofa, or coffee tables be topping them with glass, or another flat object such as an old shutter or door.

Look through your kitchen cabinets for pretty plates that could be displayed on the wall, or on an easel. It doesn't have to be in the kitchen, either!

The kitchen is also a great area to find pretty vases, cups, creamers, etc... that can be displayed on their own, or used as interesting containers for garden flowers.

Trying to add a romantic touch to your bedroom? How about displaying your wedding veil by draping it over one post of your headboard?

Also check for pretty textiles such as beaded or fringed purses to hang on the wall.

Don't forget your children's rooms. Lacy baby dresses, toddler suits or jackets can look like heritage items when hung on the wall. Simply wrap a regular hanger in ribbon or lace, and hang the garment with a picture hanger on the wall.

Have extra picture frames lying around? Use them as pretty vanity trays. Just cover the insert in a pretty fabric or paper, and lay it on a dresser for a great way to show off perfumes, candles, whatever! You could also add something personal like pressed flowers or leaves, tickets that remind you of a romantic evening, etc...

Don't be afraid to move things from other rooms if it's no longer working. The baskets you had hanging from the kitchen ceiling may look better holding towels in the guest bath. Steal a plant out of each room to make one effective grouping in the family room. That oversized chair no one sits in may be perfect in the corner of your bedroom with a throw blanket.

Got an old wooden stepladder? Use it as a plant stand, or even as an occasional table.

Finally, don't forget to look at the arrangement of your rooms. Sometimes a fresh look can be obtained simply by moving things around. We all get bored, don't let a challenged budget stop you from making your home an inviting place to be.

And now that you some basic guidelines on becoming a "budget decorator", let's get started!

Exterior Decorating on a Budget

Many times we are so busy decorating the interior of our home, we forget about the view most people see first…the outside! Perhaps we all believe improvements to the exterior of the home must be expensive. Not true! What a better place to showcase your clever creativity than where every passerby can see!

Your best friend here is a building site. Find out where they are building new homes in your area, and go talk to the contractor in charge of the site. Most of these sites have scrap piles where they discard huge amounts of materials they can't use, either because they aren't the right size, a mistake was made, or a myriad of other reasons. Ask the contractor if you can help yourself to their scrap pile, most are more than willing to let you.

Here you can find large pieces of ½ inch siding, scrap wood, broken tiles, vinyl-flooring remnants, and possibly even leftover paint or countertop material. Look at everything with the eye of the budget decorator; you can make something out of all these things!

Use the siding and scrap wood to make garden furniture, decorative shutters for your windows, or as architectural elements on your existing features. For instance, we have several large 6x6 columns on our porch, very plain lumber. We are using scrap 1x4 and 1x2 to add wrap around moldings on these columns, and painting them to contrast. It looks like a custom porch column! You could add simple shapes as appliqués to doors, gable areas, or empty walls.

Use broken tiles to make a mosaic table for the porch, or create mosaic stepping stones for the yard. You could even update a tired old picnic table with the tiles. Create a wood plaque with the scrap wood, glue or paint your house numbers on it, and add mosaic tiling around the border for a very expensive look.

If you can find a fencing company willing to give you their discards, make garden posts for hanging lanterns or plants from posts. Be sure to cement these in the ground. Use the boards to make rustic planters, or cut them down to make picket style garden fencing. Make a shingle style mailbox.

Vinyl flooring scraps can be made into floor cloths for your porch or patio with a little paint and polyurethane, and can be as decorative or as simple as you want, custom matching your homes colors and styles.

As you can see, with a little bit of hunting, you can find the materials to make the exterior of your home look like a masterpiece for almost no money, and you are saving a lot of good materials from our waste dumps!

Notes

Notes

Chapter Two

Walls and Floors

Your walls usually represent the largest space in your room, and can therefore make the most impact. The best piece of advice I can give you is-WHITE WALLS ARE BORING!

Although I occasionally see a room in white that works, give color a try, it makes such a major difference. It adds warmth and charm, in a way few other things can!

There are lots of great cures for filling those blank or boring spaces on your walls, without spending a lot of money. Remember this is a great place to show creativity and personality, so make your walls your own, and use these clever ideas as starting points to dressing your wall areas on a budget!

*Paint! Use color to transform a room. One 10-dollar can of paint will make more of a difference in a room than almost anything else. Pick your favorite color from your color scheme, (hint: It DOESN'T have to be the palest shade!) and paint your walls first, you will be inspired. Use color through your entire house, but allow for some areas for your eye to rest if you tend towards bright or rich color. If this is all you can afford to do, do this!

*Use some of the popular faux finishes for your walls.

Sponge painting is one of the easiest, requires a small amount of paint, and despite what the paint stores want you to believe, you do not have to buy an expensive sea sponge. Simply take a damp, regular household sponge, and tear little bits from the edges.

The idea is to make the shape irregular, so as not to leave any hard impressions from the edge of the sponge. Experiment on cardboard with other tools- a scrunched up plastic grocery bag, an old rag, textured fabric scraps, etc... Paint your walls the base coat of your choice, then use leftover paint for the sponging technique. I don't recommend sponging over pure white walls unless you are using a pastel shade- the contrast is just too great.

Tint leftover paint with simple acrylics, or have a small can mixed to a color somewhat lighter or darker than your base. Water down to make a wash, then dip in sponge (remove excess by blotting on paper

13

towels) and simply blot the sponge over the wall in a random pattern. This technique is also great for furniture, especially in a country or casually styled home. For an even subtler look, thin the paint with a little water. You can also use this technique right over existing paint to give it a fresh update.

For more how to's, try www.fauxlikeapro.com, www.dutchboy.com, or

www.benjaminmoore.com, or check our resource and project chapter.

*If you are having a hard time coordinating paint colors, visit your home improvement paint counters for ideas. Many paint lines have brochures or paint chip cards with pre-coordinated colors already matched for you. By the way, just because you use their cards to pick your color palette doesn't mean you have to buy their paint. Most paint companies have similar color in their lines.

*Use stencils, stamps, and sponges to create pattern. You can make simple stencil or sponge shapes yourself, or buy them relatively inexpensively if you are after something more elaborate. Use a simple shape repeated in a pattern all across a wall to simulate wallpaper. This technique uses VERY little paint, and can be quite easy on the budget, especially if you have leftover or inexpensive craft paint lying around. Watch the sales at the craft stores, you can often get craft paint for as little as 50 cents a bottle.

*Use ceiling borders to imitate architecture in your rooms. You can do this with wallpaper border, stenciling, or stamping. Simply apply your border to the area on the ceiling where the ceiling and the wall meet. You can intensify this effect by mirroring the border on the wall area adjacent to the ceiling so there is a wrap around effect.

*Another idea to enhance ceilings is to reproduce ceiling medallions around ceiling light fixtures. This works best if the light fixture is a focal point of sorts such as a chandelier, or is unusual. With a pencil, lightly draw a circle on the ceiling around the light fixture base. This is best done be removing the light fixture if it is large. An easy way to get a perfect circle is to attach your pencil to a piece of string, the hold the string at the center point of the light fixture while you draw the circle with the pencil. Holding the string tight at the right length will allow the pencil to make a perfect circle around your center point.

Now using that circle as a template, use stamps, stencils, or even decoupage elements to create a border design around the light fixture. Remember to try to repeat an element from your room theme to keep it all tied together. This will draw the eye upward in your room and give more interest to the room in general.

*Use unusual items to stamp your walls with personality. Old sneakers are great for stamping a teen's walls; an old tire with bright paint might make a great border for a boy into cars and trucks. (It doesn't have to be a straight line, either!) Cheap squishy foam balls or tennis balls make great polka dots. How about the kid's handprints in bright colors as a chair rail border? Puppy dog paws? Ok, you might have a hard time getting the family pet to cooperate on that one.

*Easy geometric sponge shapes are great for the walls of kids rooms and bathrooms. Stars, X's and O's, diamonds, etc.... They are easily cut out of ordinary household sponges. You can also pick up alphabet and numbers sponges at dollar stores meant for bath toys.

*Sponge fluffy white clouds on a blue wall, then use oval shaped sponges to sponge balloons in the sky. Use a paint pen or permanent marker to draw squiggly strings! This is terrific for a kids' bathroom or playroom, and really quick and simple.

*Write inspirational quotations on your wall with a paint pen, or even a permanent marker. Come up with your own saying, use a quote from a famous movie or book, or check out the web for ideas. www.atozquotes.com is a good place to start. Write freehand for a great hand painted look; follow chair rails or ceiling lines, or emphasize arches or unusual doorways or windows.

*Make inexpensive wall frames with foam core board and fabric scraps. Cut the desired size opening in the foam core with a craft knife, then place on a piece of fabric slightly larger than the frame. Cut an x from corner to corner INSIDE the frame opening, then use a glue gun to secure the fabric to the back of the frame. Scraps of batting used underneath the fabric can give an "upholstered" look. Or, use fabric strips to wrap around the frame over and over, securing to the back occasionally with a spot of glue. This could also work with leftover ribbon or even twine.

*Add a garden to your wall. Mask off "pickets" for a faux fence, paint in a contrasting color to the wall. Then either use purchased stamps and stencils to add vines and flowers, or make your own simple stencils from cardboard. Sunflowers, daisies, and tulips are all simple shapes. You can free hand vines with paint, or use a marker or paint pen!

*Paint your ceilings! Most people think leaving your ceilings white expands the space, but if the walls and ceiling contrast too much, the opposite occurs. A light shade of your wall color, (or a coordinating shade) on the ceiling will warm up your room considerably, and reduce that stark contrast. Also, the room just appears more finished and professional. If you have extra of the color you used on your walls, just add white paint to it until it's the desired shade, instead of going out and buying new paint. Just be sure if you used latex paint, you only add latex paint, not oil paints!!! If your ceilings are high and you want to add warmth, try a shade slightly darker than the wall color.

*Use decorative ceramic tiles to decorate your walls. Even though one might think of tiles as an expensive purchase, buying just a few for great detail decorating is very inexpensive. Use them randomly over a small wall area such as in the kitchen, or space them out around a doorway or window to bring attention. Around a fireplace surround or over a bathtub are also great ideas. Attach them to the wall with a small tube of silicone caulk you can find in the hardware section, and you won't need grout since they are being used in a decorative way. Remember, it won't take much to add a terrific accent! Look in our resources page for a ceramic dealer, or look in your local home improvement stores.

*Hang fabric on your walls. This is perfect for renters, or those who want a less permanent solution to dull walls. You can either hang fabric from a rod hung at ceiling level, or tack it in place with lathing strips you can get at you home improvement center. You can use sheets for this, and use the break between panels to hang a piece of art over the fabric. You can also hang a shelf near ceiling level, and hang the fabric from the bottom of the shelf. Don't be afraid to use paint and stamps to add pattern to the fabric if you want!

*Another non-permanent solution is to adhere fabric to your walls with liquid starch. You basically soak the fabric in the starch (you can dilute with water to make it stretch) and hang it like wallpaper, smoothing it on the wall. The great thing about this is later when you wish to change the look, just wet it, and it is easily removable. This is best done on a wall painted with gloss or semi gloss paint to prevent damage from the wet fabric. Great solution for renters.

*Don't have enough wall art? Remember, you can hang anything that appeals to you, be creative! Frame old greeting cards (especially nice if they have sentimental value), old calendar photos, pictures you like from magazines, old book photos (watch garage sales and thrift stores). Libraries sometimes have sales to raise money, and very often you can find older books you wouldn't mind tearing up for very little money.

*Need more ideas for wall art? CD covers (great for teenagers rooms), music magazines covers, seed packets, kimonos, christening gowns, baby dresses, pieces of lace, children's art, that bouquet of roses your husband sent you, favorite quilts, old love letters, gloves from your wedding day, a beaded purse, old photos picked up in antique shops (less than a dollar!), etc... Don't let traditional ideas about what should be on your walls hold you back. If something is pleasing to your eye, or holds a fond memory for you, make it a part of your home.

*Have more contemporary tastes? Simply have pieces of masonite board, (or even plywood if they won't be viewed close up) cut to size. Prime and paint them white. The take them outside with a good selection of primary colored paints and your oldest work clothes! Simply use an old paintbrush to splatter and splash paint onto the boards, modern art style. Remember, go slowly, and less is more! You may wish to allow the paint to dry some between colors. Hang these boards gallery style in any room of your home for great upscale impact!

*Learn to paint landscapes. Sound too hard, or you think you aren't artistic? Try the Bob Ross Paint Series of books, even check them out from the library if you prefer. I believe almost anyone can learn to paint landscapes with his method, and it would be a very inexpensive and personal way to fill your home with wonderful wall art. For the price of some canvas and paint, you could have paintings that might cost you hundreds apiece if you went to buy them from someone else. In addition, you may just find a lifelong pursuit and confidence from an artistic sense you didn't know you had! In addition, this same technique could be used to paint wonderful murals directly on your walls.

*Use molding in your room. Sound expensive? Use simple lathing strips and paint them your accent color. Nail them around the room at the ceiling line and at the baseboard, or use them to enclose a border at chair rail height. Your can paint, stencil, or stamp in the border, it doesn't have to be wallpaper.

*Give your room a "paneled" look by enclosing blocks of wall with lathing strips or molding, then paint or paper the interior of the "panel" a contrasting color to the wall. You can leave the "panels" as decoration themselves, or use them to showcase wall art hung inside the panels. If you don't want to budget for the border material, simply tape off the border, and paint with a color that contrasts with the background of your "paneled" wall. This is a great solution if you are trying to add color to a room without overwhelming it, or just testing out your painting confidence.

*Use leftover wallpaper, garden catalog, or even gift-wrap to decoupage a border or accent directly onto the wall. Cut out the designs you like (florals, etc.), paint the backside with Mod-Podge or white glue, and smooth onto the wall. After it dries, finish with another coat over the top to protect it. Just a warning, this is pretty permanent, although you can paint or paper OVER it later on. Hint: Use the medium with the same finish as your wall, Mod-Podge decoupage medium comes in both glossy and matte, you will have to do a test if you are using glue.

*Use contact paper as wall covering- it's cheap, and easily removed. The patterns with stripes are very easy to cut into 4-6 inch wide strips for borders. Work in lengths no longer than 3 feet so you can position them properly, or have someone help you hang them. Or hang them vertically to indicate striped wallpaper alternating with stripes of painted wall. They are paper backed, so you can measure and draw cutting lines on the back if your pattern choice is not a stripe. Cut the pieces one half inch too long, then let them shrink for a week or two before you do the final trim, and don't stretch it while your hanging, or it will shrink even more. Or trace shapes on the paperback, cut them out, and place around the room in a regular or random pattern. You could take a shape from a pattern already in the room to co-ordinate. Other ideas are simple stars, flowers, hearts, cars (child's room), etc... Try highlighting mantels, important artwork, arches, windows, or other focus points. Or how about spelling out your child's name on the wall or window?

*Start a collection of inexpensive antiques for a wall display. Silverware, utensils, photos, postcards, keys, garden implements etc. can all be found at antique shops for very little money. Group them together on a wall for the best impact. Vintage doilies and quilts can often be found cheaply if the have some damage, but there is almost always a way to hang or display an item to showcase it's best features.

*Looking for an eye catching way to hang the family photos? How about a family tree? Paint a large tree on your wall with spreading branches. This doesn't have to be an elaborate painting, just the basics will do! Don't use paints that are too bright, use realistic greens and browns from nature. When its dry go back with a small brush and some ivory paint and lay little lines of highlights along the trunk and branches where the light might hit it. If there is a window in the room, use the direction of the light source to guide which side of the trunk to put highlights. Make sure there are enough branches for each family member to have their own, and pets too if you wish. Then simply hang each family member's photos up along their branch...mine starts with the youngest photo on the bottom, and works upward to the most recent. You could even use a paint pen to label your tree..."The Wilson Family Tree" or dates if you prefer. Remember, it's just paint. If you change your décor down the road, it can be easily painted over!

*Use the same stencils or stamps you used in the rest of your room to create a picture on fabric, frame and hang. Or stamp the matting of artwork in the room to coordinate.

*Make an herb and flower drying rack out of lathing strip or scrap wood and some small nails or cup hooks, gather herbs and flowers from your garden or nearby fields and display on the rack while they dry. It's best to secure the ends with rubber bands so as the stems dry and shrink, the rubber bands will hold tight. You can cover the rubber bands with ribbon if you like. This rack can be as small or large as you wish, or can be made to fit a narrow area such as above a doorway or archway.

*Get a large framed mirror look on the wall over the mantel without the framed mirror price. Mount a bathroom type plain mirror over the mantel with mirror clips, and then hang a swag of fabric to drape over the top and sides of the mirror. Accessories on the mantel will hide any mirror clips showing along the bottom. Be sure to follow instructions on the clip package so the mirror will be secure.

*You *can* successfully use those self-stick mirror tiles that were so popular in the 1970's. Mount the tiles on a wall or a board leaving the width of a lathing strip between them. Nail lathing strip between the tiles and around the edge to create a "window" mirror!

*Make plain plywood boxes that can be painted and mounted on the wall as stunning wall art display surfaces. Hint: The home center will do all the cutting for you for a small fee! Be sure to anchor the boxes to wall studs or use wall anchors from the hardware store.

Use the same boxes or even just small blocks of wood screwed to the wall to place small candles on...the whole wall will glow when they are lit. This is unbelievable in a bathroom or dining room. Just make sure nothing is mounted above them, and that no flammable material such as a curtain that could catch fire.

*The trick to hanging baskets on the wall and making it work? Hang LOTS of them, and group them together! Vary the shapes and textures, and let them contrast with the wall. Try hanging them in tight groups along and over wide doorways, such as that space between a kitchen and dining area.

*Make your own picture frame. Try just gluing together four twigs for a rustic look, make bread dough frames and paint them to match your room (glue a picture hanger to the back) or simply paint a frame directly on the wall. If you know how to use a miter box saw (and it's a cinch to learn), you can learn to create beautiful wood frames from cheap pine boards.

*Make a French bulletin board for hanging your snapshots, bills and correspondence. Cut a sheet of sturdy cardboard to your desired size. Cut a piece of 1-inch thick foam to the same size. Choose a piece of fabric to cover the board, and cut slightly larger so that you can wrap it around and hot glue it to the back. Now use ribbon to cross over the board both directions about 4 inches apart. Weave the ribbon where it meets. Hot glue the ends of the ribbon on the backside of the board. Now you can slip your photos behind the ribbons, or use pins to secure items into the foam like a bulletin board. This is a great idea over a kitchen desk, and much prettier than a traditional bulletin board.

*Show your patriotic spirit. Save pictures of American flags from magazine covers, newspapers, you can even download them from the Internet. Frame them in inexpensive frames, and group them together on a wall by themselves in memory of all those who have fallen for our great country.

*Dress up your current frames for a detail that can't be missed! Your glue gun will come in handy here! You can glue a variety of items to your frames to make them one of a kind. Small pinecones, seashells, buttons, pasta, coffee beans, driftwood pieces, bottle caps, wine corks, wood cutouts, small novelty toys- the list is endless! Arrange the items in patterns or randomly on paper first before you start gluing. Try combining more than one item on the same frame. Try working out a theme to the picture or your décor; pencils and erasers on school pictures, fishing lures or flies on vacation photos, found sea glass from that great day at the beach. If you have a military man in the family, how about accenting the frames with small army soldiers or toy boats?

*One large piece of art can make more impact, and has a simpler, cleaner look than several smaller ones. If your art piece is meant to be a focal point, don't make it share the wall and it will give you more impact.

*Make fabric ribbons to hang behind pictures. The picture is not suspended from the ribbon, it just is meant to appear that way. This is a great way to add color to a wall. You can also use hemmed fabric strips from other fabric projects in the room.

*Use a sponge cut into a square to add a checkerboard pattern as a border. You can use one paint color, or two to create the pattern. This technique lends itself well to imitating rustic mosaic tile... simply leave a slight space between tiles to indicate grout, and remember that the background color will be your grout color. Another option would be to imitate bricks or stones. Dipping the paint in 2 or 3 different colors before stamping best does this. As always, be sure you don't have too much paint on the sponge by doing a test print first on paper.

*Wallpaper with unique items- maps, old love letters, travel posters, music posters, and old bookplates. You can either use decoupage medium or wallpaper paste, I find the former a little easier. If your item is thick or heavy, try using wallpaper paste designed for vinyl wallpaper.

*Make a beautiful replica of those expensive French wall clocks that are all the rage. Purchase a plywood round and a battery operated clock kit from your hardware store. We're probably talking less than $10 here. Find the center of the clock by drawing two intersecting lines, and then drill a hole large enough to fit through the clock hand. Sand, prime, and paint the clock a beige or off white color. Use decoupage to add florals, beautiful foreign scenes or even favorite animals. This is one of those times that catalogs, calendars, and vacation brochures come in handy. Now add numbers! You can hand paint, use stick on numbers, or just use simple dots. Just be sure to mark them in pencil first until you have the placement correct. If that becomes too complicated, just place a dot at 12,3,6, and 9. Rub the whole piece with wood stain to antique it, and then add the clock mechanism. Voila! Or, whatever the French would say here!

*Embellish all your existing linens with your personal touch. Add ribbon, fabric appliqués, beads, paint or tassels to dress up your towels, bedding, placemats, napkins, tablecloths, and curtains.

*Find a great place to hang your children's art (I have

5 to 8 kids at my house at any one time, no frig is THAT big!) How about string a clothesline across a playroom wall, then clip artwork all the way across the wall with clothespins? Or paint a wall with a base coat of magnetic paint, and make a whole wall your refrigerator? Magnetic paint can be found at home improvement stores.

*Need a large floor cloth, but can't afford a large rug? Find a clearance piece of vinyl flooring in your home center (I found mine for 6 bucks) and paint the wrong side a base coat color. You may want to consider priming it first, I prime everything now. Use stamps or stencils to add your design, and you have a custom floor cloth. The most expensive part of the project will be sealing it with polyurethane; it will probably need 4-6 coats. I've heard of a few people who have had success sealing it with paste wax, but I wouldn't depend on that unless it wouldn't get a lot of traffic or spills.

*Another use for a painted floor cloth? How about a hopscotch pattern for the playroom, or a racetrack or city streets for your son or daughters room? It's also a great idea for outdoor rooms such as your porch or patio.

*Since we're on floors, did you know you *can* paint that hideous 1970's floor? Seal first with a good primer sealer made for non-porous surfaces, (BIN or KILZ are good brands) and then simply paint with regular household latex in any pattern or color. Try a checkerboard, or simple contrasting border, or even borders around furniture arrangements! Keep in mind, this kind of limits your re-arranging abilities! You can use stencils and stamps, or simply mask off your areas. When it is thoroughly dry, seal and protect it with 4-6 coats of water based polyurethane. Use more polyurethane in higher traffic areas.

*If you have older throw rugs that bore you, there is no reason you can't dress them up or bring them into the style of your room. Sew a fabric border all around the edges, or use paint to stamp a design onto the rug itself. Use fabric paint or buy a product called textile medium to add to regular craft or house paint to soften the feel of the paint and make it more permanent. You could even add fringe to the edges with a large upholstery needle and some yarn or floss. Simply use the needle to pull the floss halfway through on the edge of the rug, then tie the ends together. Repeat all the way across the end of the rug. When you are finished, use sharp scissors to even out the ends of the fringe.

*Shop for frames at garage sales. Even if it's the tackiest picture in the world, the frame may be well worth the measly buck you just paid for it! Remember, the frame can be painted, too.

* How about a coat of paint? Bring a roomful of mismatched frames together by painting them all the same color. This is also a great place to try out a new faux finishing technique- if you make a mistake; it takes very little paint to start over!

* Learn to quilt, and make a simple wall quilt to hang. Try a memory quilt, and make each square out of a treasured piece of your children's clothing or blankets. It doesn't have to be elaborate; a simple block quilt can be quite effective. There are many books at the library available for free use, and it is much easier than you think if you keep to beginner's projects. Quilts can also become lasting family heirlooms, so give it a try!

*Save and frame colorful labels for a contemporary and colorful wall display for your kitchen. Soup cans and cereal boxes have always been favorites. The trick is to look for graphic designs with good contrast, and group several together to make it look deliberate.

*Decoupage seed packets in a border at your ceiling line to make a great colorful "garden" statement. You could also cut pictures out of free garden catalogs when you are done ordering for the year.

*Use the salt dough recipe from the accessories chapter to make wall plaques you can hang. Cut out simple pots, leaves, and flowers (or come up with your own theme or scene) and layer them together on a cookie sheet. Bake them as one piece at 250 degrees, checking them every 15 to 30 minutes. Be aware the thicker pieces may require more baking time. When they are thoroughly dry, paint and seal them. You don't have to be realistic with the paint; just some casual washes with pale or pastel colors will give an elegant watercolor look. Using a hot glue gun, glue a picture hanger to the backside. Hang in groups for a "collection" effect, or over a doorway or around a window.

*Decorative items don't have to fit in a frame to be great wall art. Paint an old wooden board with thoughtful prose, hang a wooden ladder and use it as a display shelf, and tools or farm implements are an old favorite. A section of charming fence, an old window, even a piece of interesting molding off an old house can be real eye catchers, and add a sense of history.

*Create your own piece of architectural salvage that is so hot in the decorating scene today. You can pick up new garden ornaments for a fraction of what you would pay at a flea market for the real thing, and then use paint finishes to age the piece. Lattice, wood panels and other wood pieces can be found at your lumberyard or home improvement center. You'll find directions foe a crackle finish in the project chapter of this book, or simply paint a wood piece with paint thinned with water as a wash, then sand areas to make the piece look old. Rub with some wood stain and you have a very "chic" ornament for your home!

* Make nature prints on fabric or paper, then frame. You can actually use a real leaf, fern frond, or flower, lightly paint one side, and then gently press onto your surface. Try several test prints first, and experiment with adding several colors at once. This procedure works best if there isn't too much paint, so blot on a paper towel first so you get a better image.

I hope this inspires you to bring your imagination to your walls. Remember, even though these projects are quite inexpensive, or even free, the best thing about them will be the personality you impart with them in decorating your home!

Painted surfaces are one of the hottest decorating trends today, with faux finished walls right up there at the top. Take some time to learn them, they are easy, inexpensive, and can make a dramatic difference in your home.

Use these ideas as a jumping off point. Remember, you can make the most dramatic impact in a room by decorating one of the largest visual areas...the walls.

Try this exercise.

Walk through your home and find the room that most screams out...BORING WALLS! Make a commitment to paint or faux finish that one room as your next project. Pick a color or finish that you absolutely love, and remember to stay within the style of your room. For instance, if your room style is farmhouse country, a marbleized wall probably isn't going to look right! When your done, I think the drama of the improvement will be just the inspiration you need to lead you into more decorating projects...and it will impose a sense of confidence that you may not have even realized was lacking before. And remember, the worst thing that can happen is that you don't like it; the nice thing about paint is that you can paint it again!

Notes

Notes

Chapter Three

Accessories and Furniture

This is perhaps my favorite stage in decorating, and also where you may become the most creative. Use these ideas to add clever touches, personal ambiance, and eye catching final touches to your rooms!

*Disguise votive candles or votive holders with organic material to dress them up. Use that glue gun, add cinnamon sticks, fat twigs from the yard, old potpourri, pressed leaves, cloves, interesting seed pods, even buttons or pasta for a contemporary approach! If you want to glue things directly to the candle, try also tying it with raffia, just in case the heat of the flame loosens the glue you use. If you desire, you can dip the candle after in melted paraffin or candle wax to seal the items into the candle. Use an old coffee can to melt the wax; you will never get it out of a pot! This is a great way to update your candles for the summer!

Always make sure to keep all decoration away from the flame area. This is a great way to add freshness to candles in the summer, instead of having to put them away!

*Make small picture frames out of the same bread dough your kids play with! It can be painted after it's baked, and you can even bake a small picture hanger right onto the back, or glue one on later. Try making a circular or rectangular frame, and then arrange small cutouts on it before you bake, such as hearts, stars, etc... Paint it gold when it's hard, and you'll have a gorgeous designer frame for the price of flour!

Here are two different dough recipes...give each a try to see which works best for you.

Bread dough recipe:
2 Cups Flour
½ Cup Salt
1 tsp. Vegetable oil
A Tablespoon of water at a time until it is a non-sticky dough consistency

Bake at 250F until hard and slightly golden, times vary with size, check after first hour, and then every 15 minutes.

Soda Clay Recipe
1-Cup Baking Soda
½ Cup Cornstarch
¾ Cup water

Cook on low heat until thick, approximately 7-10 minutes. Be sure to keep stirring those last minutes to keep it as smooth as possible. Turn out onto a board and knead with more cornstarch as necessary until the right consistency. Air-dry your pieces until completely dry before painting.

Use these same recipes to dress up shelf brackets, door and window frames, and moldings. Try using a cake-decorating bag to create more detailed designs, baking them and painting, then attaching them with a glue gun to surfaces.

*Use old flannel or oxford shirts to recover a chair seat. Button up the shirt, and then cut the material so the buttons run up the middle of the seat. You may wish to sew a seam right up the middle to keep the shirt permanently closed in the case a button was lost. You can do the same with a seat of a pair of jeans, pockets and all. This touch is whimsical and clever!

*If you are tired of that boring bath mirror, but can't afford to replace it with a large framed mirror, try hanging a swag of fabric over it. Place small hooks or holders at the top corners of the mirror and pull your fabric through. Make sure the fabric strip is long enough to cascade down both sides of the mirror to the countertop. This will go a long way to softening your bathroom and adding much needed style! Try coordinating the fabric with the shower curtain fabric.

*Watch end of the season sales for garden lanterns for unusual indoor lighting. The electric type can be hung in the place of chandeliers or other hanging fixtures on a chain, and since they don't require a professional install, you can use them anywhere. The candle variety is a great accent for over an entry table or a dining room side table.

*Update old picture frames by gluing them with…anything! Old buttons, pasta, seashells, string, nuts and bolts, seed pods, little toys…

anything that is appropriate to your room. You can paint the whole frame after it dries if you wish.

*Got tired old end tables? Cover them with a swath of fabric; tuck ends under in a casual "pouf" and you have new tables, no sewing. As an extra, you can store things under the table, and no one will know! Try layering several different fabrics for a lush, romantic look.

*You can update an old dresser by covering the drawer fonts with fabric. Remove the drawers from the dresser, and take off all the hardware. Measure the size of the drawer front, and cut your chosen fabric an inch or two larger. To make a really professional look, cut pieces of batting or old blanket the same size as the drawer fronts. Now layer first the batting, then the fabric over the front, use a staple gun to staple it onto the backside of the drawer front. Now poke a hole with a scissors so you can replace the hardware. Try combining this technique with paint...paint the rest of the dresser one of the colors from your chosen fabric for a designer look.

*Create a modern end table with copper pipe. You will need a small pipe cutter, which is easy to use. Cut the pipe to make a frame for a block the size of the table you desire, and use copper elbows to connect all the ends. Ask your home improvement store for suggestions on what type of adhesive would be best for you. Top the table with a round of glass you can get at any discount store. Alternatively, you could create the same table from pvc pipe, then spray paint it copper.

*Grow fast growing plants from cuttings. Ask a friend if you can borrow a couple of stems, or take cuttings from the ivy in the yard. Let them sit in water until you see roots, then pot up for free houseplants. Experiment with several, but remember if you are trying outdoor plants to grow indoors, choose shade loving varieties as indoor light is much lower in intensity.

*Buy flowering shade annuals in six packs- they grow fast, are very cheap, and make great houseplants, even into winter. Impatiens, fuchsias, and begonias are all good choices and are available nationwide.

*If you are lucky enough to have paneled doors in your house, tape off the panels and paint the interior to coordinate with the room. For a very elegant traditional look, rag the panels with a warm earth tone wash. This wash can be made by mixing your paint with equal parts of glaze, or just mix the paint with a little water, but work fast!

The water wash is cheaper, but dries much faster so you don't have as much time to work with the paint.

*Decoupage pretty gift-wrap in blocks over the frame of a wall mirror. Hey, an actual good reason to save that gift-wrap! Make sure you remove the frame from the mirror first, and overlap the blocks of paper slightly. If you do happen to get glue onto the glass, wait until it dries and scrape it off with a razor blade.

*Use those cheap ugly utility pots, but group them together in a large planter or basket. Or simply allow the foliage to hide the pot sides, place trailing plants on the outer edge of the grouping. Use small boxes or overturned pots to add varying height. Or, paint those reusable containers. Half my container garden is planted in plastic kitty litter buckets!

*If you have an old aquarium lying around, or see one cheap at a garage sale, turn it into a plant paradise! Create a terrarium by adding a layer of gravel to the bottom for drainage before you add soil. Place in your plants, driftwood, rocks, or whatever you want to create a miniature world. The light tube that comes with most aquariums can be fitted with any broad-spectrum fluorescent bulb. (It doesn't have to be an expensive "plant" bulb.) Water when the soil at the surface feels dry to the touch. This could potentially be done on a grand scale with a large aquarium for an outstanding focal point in a room. Often aquariums that have been scratched can be gotten for a song at pet stores or through classified ads.

*Do you have an old wooden ladder that is no longer safe? Use it as a great plant stand, either inside or out. You can paint it if you wish, or leave it rustic if that fits in with your style. Place pots on the steps, and hang small plant baskets from the rungs and supports.

* There are several ways to make your bed a focal point of the room without spending a fortune. Try using a stencil to give the impression of a headboard. You can tailor the deign to match your room, even imitate an elegant wood or iron headboard if you wish, but also try less obvious solutions, such as a cluster of birdhouses or sports equipment for a boys room.

Fabric is a very elegant way to set off your bed, either hang an entire panel shirred on a rod behind the bed, or perhaps just a swag of leftover fabric will do. The higher you hang the panel, the more emphasis you give the bed in the room.

Finally, you can easily make a headboard out of a piece of plywood. Simply cover the plywood with fabric and a staple gun...use batting (or an old blanket or comforter) under the fabric to give it an upholstered look. Don't worry about the back; no one will see the staple job. You can also paint the headboard; this can be great for a kid's room, as you can match their decor. How about a castle or a playhouse motif? Use your imagination and you'll never know you didn't spend a fortune on a custom treatment!

*Learn to make slipcovers! Recovering chair seats is as easy as a staple gun, and you can make casual slipcovers for furniture with fusible hem tape if you don't sew. Check out the project chapter for easy instructions. Also consider making slipcovers for your throw pillows, they add a great accent.

You can also make a slipcover of sorts for your bedroom comforter. This can be a way to change inexpensively for the seasons, or to re-do a room altogether. Take two flat sheets the same size as your comforter, and sew together leaving one of the short ends open. Using buttons, Velcro, or snaps, create a closure along that open side. Now place your comforter inside the cover like a giant pillowcase, and you have a brand new bedroom ensemble!

*Use those leftover scraps to make colorful patchwork placemats. It's as simple as sewing squares of fabric in rows, then hemming the edges. Why not make matching potholders while you're at it? Make several sets in different colors that coordinate with your kitchen. Consider making a holiday set too!

*Hang fabric panels at doorways and room divisions to add softness and style, and to help make that definition from room to room. You could use inexpensive muslin, or simply buy a twin sheet, cut it in half lengthwise, hem, and hang from small cup hooks and ribbon. The hooks can suspend either from the ceiling or the wall, and the ribbon loops can be sewn on by hand, with a machine, or fused with hem tape. Other options would be stapling fabric to the back of lathing strip and nailing in place, or sewing small casings in the fabric, inserting a dowel, and suspending the dowel from the ceiling with ribbon and hooks. You could also use short curtain rods, but why not be creative?

*You can make your own throw rugs by pulling strips of fabric through rug meshing in a variety of ways, then sealing the bottom with fusible interfacing. This is a great project for thrift store clothing and fabric, or even out of your own closet. See our project chapter for more specific instructions.

*Give your daughter a canopy bed without the expense. The idea is to give the illusion of a canopy. Fabric can be swagged over the bed using common ceiling hooks; the kind people hang plants from. I used simple eyebolts with pound in type wall anchors. Or install a café curtain rod or towel rings on the ceiling at both the head and foot of the bed, and drape a canopy of fabric over each rod, allowing it to dip in the middle. Install one hook in the ceiling near the center of the bed, and hang 4 panels long enough to drape over the posts on the bed. Hang a shelf over the head of the bed, and staple fabric panels to the top of the shelf.

*Use small grapevine wreaths as tiebacks for curtains, or as swag holders. Dress them up by gluing on leftover dried flowers, beads, shells, etc... Try using several together, similar to how a woman might wear multiple bangle bracelets on her arm.

*Make memory frames. Line a picture frame with felt, and then fill with memories of a special occasion. Ticket stubs and a program from your daughter's recital, old love letters and a hotel key from your honeymoon, mementos from a family vacation. These are the types of personal touches that make your home warm and special to those who live there.

*Use old blankets or mattress pads as batting for your quilted projects- placemats, table runners, quilts, baby blankets. These are easy and cheap to get at thrift stores or garage sales, too. Check with relatives and friends, they might have old ones they are getting ready to throw out or donate. Wash in your machine first, and be sure to put them through the dryer for at least 20 minutes.

*Wrap an extra fabric piece around a boring lamp base and tie with cording, ribbon, or raffia. This can be a coordinating leftover from a fabric project in the room, or a neutral fabric from the clearance table at the fabric store. This is also another great use for old curtain material or bedspreads.

*To make a dramatic change in your kitchen, paint those cabinets. Unless you're lucky enough to have beautiful wood finish cabinets, nothing can make more of a difference then some sandpaper, good scrubbable paint, and some elbow grease!

You can also paint those ugly kitchen countertops. First, get a good quality primer made specifically for non-porous surfaces. BIN or KILZ are what I recommend. Follow the directions to get a good primer coat down. Now the fun part! Here's where you get to use those great faux finishing techniques we've been talking about. Learn how to marbleize, or use a faux stone finish on the countertops. ALWAYS practice first! When your entire look is done and dry, seal the countertops liberally. I would recommend 4-6 coats of a water-based polyurethane. With a little care this should last you quite a long time. Hint: If you want those high gloss finishes from the magazine pages, go ahead and use gloss polyurethane...just be aware it will show every smear and smudge in the right light!

*Make simple stencils from cardboard, or re-use the plastic "board" that comes with bacon. Save those cereal boxes and shirt stuffers!

*Use marbleizing and other faux finishes as a way of disguising damaged furniture or updating old and boring pieces. I recently picked up a solid oak Queen Anne style coffee table at a garage sale for $10. (Totally worth it since they threw in a solid silver candy dish for free, but that's another story.) I sanded down the top, filled the dents with wood putty, and marbleized it with several shades of earthy green. Everyone who has walked in my door 100% believes that to be an authentic Victorian antique marble table. The same could be done for contemporary tables from the 1980's that have lost their style impact, or even to a simple plywood cube!

*Use attractive books for display. Nothing adds more charm and easy style. Stack three or four books on the coffee table and top with a container of flowers...stack them in the bookcase in several areas to offer a much more pleasant arrangement than just rows and rows of books...stack them on the mantle, even use hardback books to make an end table! Glue together four stacks of hardback books to equal heights, and simply top with a round of glass. Books for this purpose can be found for pennies at garage sales, thrift stores, and library sales.

*Sponge paint accessories with pastel paint for a "graniteware" effect. Blues, greens, and roses are popular sponge ware colors. This can include everything from pitchers and dishware (use paint made fro glassware) to furniture pieces such as tables, dining chairs, or desk accessories.

*Make a "candle chandelier"! Get a large grapevine wreath, and attach three or four lengths of chain, similar to how you would hang a hanging light fixture. Use floral wire to attach small clay pots upright to the wreath, and pop votive candles into the pots. Use your imagination and your glue gun to decorate the wreath, and then hang it low over a table, or forget the chain and use it as a table wreath centerpiece! Please be very careful no ignitable items come in contact with the candles, and that the candleholders are tightly secured.

You can use this same technique to make a hanging pot rack for your kitchen. Use a sturdy large wreath, and just attach s-hooks to the bottom. Still feel free to add embellishments to dress up the rack, or wrap with some silk vine, dried flowers or herbs, garlic, and so on. I wouldn't hang cast iron from this, however!

Another idea for a great unique pot rack? Hang an old iron wine rack from the ceiling with chain and anchor hooks. Provide large s-hooks to hang the pots and utensils from.

*If you have beautiful jewelry you would like to display, why not hang it right on the wall? A few cup hooks over a dressing table and voila! This would be great for displaying jewelry of great sentimental value, such a Grandmother's pearl necklace or earrings.

*Decoupage accessories to give them new life. Pressed flowers, magazine photos, garden catalogs, gift wrap, fabric etc. can be used to dress up picture frames, lamps and shades, tables, pots or buckets, switch plates, the list goes on! Just brush white glue or decoupage medium onto the back of your materials and glue in place. When it is completely dry, brush on an all over coat of glue to seal, allow it to dry thoroughly, and enjoy! Here's a tip; if you decoupage with fabric, brush a layer of glue over the fabric and let dry before you cut it out-this will help your fabric lay better, and prevent it from fraying. Also, use a cotton fabric, as it accepts the glue more readily.

*Make plantscapes! Use houseplants or flowering annuals in unusual containers for charm and impact. Buckets, wooden boxes, birdcages, teapots, even old boots can make personal statements. Just be sure to line your container with plastic if it is not waterproof, and allow for drainage for the plant. Also, try combining more than one type of plant in a container for contrast. Make sure to use plants for low light situations if it will not be placed near a bright window.

*Spray paint pinecones and hang from light fixture and curtain rods. Great in a "natural" theme. Acorns and seedpods work too, but you may have to use a glue gun to attach the hanging cord.

*Ideas for inexpensive beds? Frames and box springs for beds can be quite costly, but there are some alternatives. First, don't let anybody convince you that you are not doing your job if your kids aren't sleeping on the newest deluxe bed set from the nearest furniture store. For centuries many Asian cultures have slept on a mat on the floor…and are probably the better for it with healthier backs, and a healthier sense of the material world.

However, there are several ideas you can use either temporarily or as permanent solutions.

Simply create a plywood platform or box just slightly larger than your mattress. Paint, and then place the mattress on the platform. You could create a platform that is somewhat longer than the mattress, the extra space to be used as a bed table.

Use a standard metal frame, but fit the bottom with plywood or scrap 2x4, and lay the mattress directly on that. This, after all, is the theory behind futons.

Buy a futon mattress, but leave the frame until later. The cushion can be folded in half against a wall during the day to use as seating.

Place a sheet of ¾ inch plywood on top of concrete blocks…lay a bed skirt over the wood and place the mattress.

*Use those inexpensive cotton throw rugs as table runners…they are much sturdier and cheaper, and you can often find them on clearance. You can wash them in the washer, and then place them in the dryer on low temperature.

*To give a serving or display bowl more importance, place it on top of an overturned bowl or dish of the same size or slightly larger. This can be very effective to raise a flower arrangement to the scale of the table.

*Use common stones found in your garden or around your neighborhood to dress up floral displays, or on their own in attractive bowls. Simply place a small bowl of stones next to a flower display for instant organic chemistry. Attractive stones can be displayed on their own, especially if you have contrasting colors that can be grouped together.

Here's a great and easy display option. Make three shallow wooden boxes, each a couple of inches smaller than the next. Nest the boxes inside each other, filling the extra space in the bottom two boxes with pretty stones. Now plant the top box with attractive houseplants, and a few more stones.

*Make ingenious occasional tables out of found items. Top an old birdbath with a round of glass. (The kind the discount stores sell for their 3-legged pressboard tables, about 3 bucks) How about two large clay pots, epoxied end to end, and topped with glass? I have filled old five gallon buckets with some gravel to weigh them down, covered them with a pouf of fabric, and topped with a round of glass with great success! If you can't, or choose not to use glass, try covering a plywood round with fabric and a staple gun. I've even used a round marble cutting board!

*Tie colorful squares of fabric over jar and canister lids in the kitchen for a splash of color. (Hint: Rubber bands hold them on best, you can tie or glue on pretty ribbon over it.)

*Hot glue decorative items to existing cabinet pulls to add flair or change the feel in a room. Seashells, polished stones, or beads are good starter ideas.

*Hang those cheap roll up matchstick style blinds as room dividers. Most home improvement stores sell an inexpensive vinyl variety. Hanging them from the ceiling is just as easy as hanging them from the wall, just follow the manufacturer's instructions. This is a great idea for shared kid's rooms, or for bedrooms with a home office.

*Sew placemats together with floss or even leather strips to make a long runner. Try using the organic weave kind from the import store to create a one of a kind throw rug.

*Stitch up simple square potholders either in a solid color to work with your kitchen, or in a patchwork checkerboard pattern, and hang them near the stove. Insert a small piece of ribbon into the last seam as a hanging loop.

*If a beautiful armoire or TV cabinet is out of your budget, here's how to create one you can definitely afford. Watch garage sales or the newspaper for an old storage cabinet. You know the kind, the laminate variety the discount stores sell? If you are going to use it for a TV, be sure to measure the inside to make sure it is deep enough. Invest in a couple of dollars worth of crown molding and add it to the top of the piece (pre drill your holes to prevent splitting), or trim out the edges and doors with molding or lathing strip. Sand and prime well with a non-porous primer such as BIN. Now take your time and develop a plan for decorative painting that will wow everyone you know! Watch magazines, there are always several painted cabinets in every issue I read; you can copy ideas from them. Combine several different techniques…ragging, decoupage, sponging, stamping, or crackle finishes. Create "panels" within the doors with paint. Add feet purchased from the lumber section of your home improvement store. Paint the interior one of the accent colors in your design. Splurge on a nice set of hardware. Take your time, and it will look like you paid thousands for it!

*Use plants! The secret to making an impact with them is to use several large plants, or group smaller ones together instead of spreading them throughout the house. Try using boxes to add varying height, the foliage will disguise them.

*Trim furniture to be painted with wood molding to add great detail. The molding doesn't have to be expensive, lathing strips will do. Pre-drill the holes to prevent the molding from splitting. If it's an important piece of furniture, spend a few bucks on some cool crown molding for the top of the piece. It doesn't take much and makes a world of difference.

*Cover sturdy cardboard boxes with fabric, ribbon, contact paper or accessories and use them for table displays. They can add height to plants or bric-brac, or act as decorative holders for planting pots, as storage for small items, etc…

*Save pretty bottles and display in a sunny window. Fill clear glass with colored water to co-ordinate with the room. You can pick up corks at the craft store to make them look more stylish and authentic.

*Turn your dining room light fixture into something special by hanging ornaments from it with clear thread. Pinecones, strings of beads, silk vines, and dried flower bunches, even antique silverware! Use whatever compliments your decor.

*Hang a tiered vegetable basket from the ceiling in your shower. This is a great way to store all of your sundries, and will be hidden from view by the shower curtain or door. As a bonus, you can often pick them up at the dollar store for…yep, you guessed it, a buck!

*Spray paint small clay pot saucers as great coasters. Use painted clay pots to hold silverware, napkins, or packets of condiments. By the way, they *can* go through the dishwasher!

*Use local vegetation. Find whatever plant is available to you locally in abundance, (and usually free) and use it very deliberately in a large-scale display. Some of the more architectural plants like horsetail look great this way. Make sure you have permission before you collect from someone's property, and don't collect protected species. A call to your local cooperative extension office ought to put you on the right track.

*Easy upholstered headboards? Just cover a large piece of plywood with batting and fabric using a staple gun. Use a glue gun to attach buttons, cording or ribbon if you desire. Or fuse felt animals onto the fabric before you attach for a great child's room accent. Now, simply attach to the bed frame with screws, or just sandwich the headboard between the bed and wall, screw to wall studs if it's large or heavy. (By the way, if this is for a young child, be careful what you glue on!)

*Make "nature" prints. Use fabric paint and actual vegetables or plant matter to stamp accents on dishtowels, aprons, or even scrap fabric, and then frame it! An apple cut in half; an artichoke, carrot, pinecone, even sturdy herbs and flowers can be dabbed with paint and used as stamps! Try using a marker to add accents after it dries, such as stems or seeds.

*Use inexpensive (about 20 cents each) small grapevine wreaths as napkin rings, slipped over candles as a base, grouped in rows above a doorway, or glue on decorative accents as "mini" wreaths.

*Use inexpensive closet dowelling found at home improvement stores to hang curtains, bed canopies, and fabric on walls. Or as pot racks or organizational racks. It can be cut to any size and can be hung from the ceiling with chain, or attached to the walls with simple brackets. It can even be shirred with fabric or painted!

*Use old favorite sweaters as material for throw pillow covers… what a great way to personalize your home, and keep a favorite piece of clothing close by! This is also great for a child who just can't let go of that ratty old piece of clothing, a great compromise for Mom!

*Add appliqués in various shapes to pillow covers to add detail, or to bring the pillow into the theme of a room. A simple zigzag stitch on most sewing machines around the edge of the appliqué will do the job, or use a no fray material like felt and slipstitch or glue into place. Sew on buttons or beads, both can be found at garage sales. Never overlook the "free" box at garage sales…it might just be that the trims you find will definitely be worth the price! Also keep your eyes out for useable fabric…there may be a major tear or stain somewhere, but if there is enough usable fabric that you like to cover a picture frame, why not?

*Don't have time to make slipcovers for all your dining room chairs? Just make a small slipcase to slide over the top of the chair back, similar to a short pillowcase, to dress it up and add color.

*Use a simple yard of beautiful cording (you find on sale of course) to hang over a bed, a doorway, or a vignette you wish to set off. It could be a wall art grouping, or a tablescape you are especially proud of.

*Decoupage clear plates on the backside, then paint a background color over the decoupage, and you have great decorative plates to display on racks or on the wall, for around a buck apiece. You could even decoupage color copies of photos for a unique way to display family treasures!

* Need a computer or office desk, cheap? Take two metal file cabinets, and spray paint them the same color. Use a hollow core door, or a sheet of plywood as the tabletop, and finish it out with wood molding along the outer three edges for a great custom look. (Hint: pre-drill the holes before you nail on the molding to prevent it from splitting.) Paint the top; try a faux stone finish for a really great elegant look. Try finishing out your nearby bookcases or other furniture in matching molding, and painting them to co-ordinate. A beautiful office suite at a fraction of the price!

*Use fresh flowers in every room of your house! You don't need expensive containers, any coffee cup, pitcher, or glass bottle will do. Roadside daisies will do the job, forget those expensive floral shops. Few things make such a romantic statement in the home.

Try repeating a simple flower holder en masse to make a provocative statement. A windowsill with nine or ten matching objects with flowers makes quite a scene.

*Make cabinet hardware with polymer clay, a new bakeable clay found in craft stores. You can insert a screw into your creation before you bake it. There are actually many great books out now on the use of polymer clay, try checking a few out of the library for more ideas.

*Use photo transfer paper to make memory pillows, quilts, or wall hangings. This very cool product found in craft stores allows you to transfer a color copy of a photograph to fabric using an iron, just like the old iron on transfers we all used to use. Make a panel with photos of your loved ones, and sew it into accessories for your home. This makes a really great gift for grandparents too. I also think it would be terrific to help a baby with separation anxiety, or a child whose parent must travel could keep a pillow with their picture on it.

*Grow some flowers from seed for your vases. Seed is very cheap, and all you need is a small plot of land, (tucked in among your shrubs is fine) some sun, and water. Sunflowers, zinnias, cosmos, and wildflower mixes practically grow themselves!

*Don't put away the vases in winter. Fill your vases with potpourri, then tuck in interesting branches and twigs...bigger is better. This looks great against the contrast of a white wall.

*Try your hand at paper mache. Use one of the recipes in the projects chapter to create one of a kind artwork and accessories. All you need is newspapers, some household items, some imagination and time. In addition to bowls or vases, try creating paper mache fruit, flowers, fish, or other theme related accessory.

*Make organic ornaments. Cover Styrofoam balls (or old tennis balls, baseballs, etc, that are past their prime) with moss, coffee beans, dried beans, dried flower petals, small pine cones, small shells, whatever you have, and display them grouped in bowls, or hung from thread from a window or light fixture. Use hot glue for the heavier items, but white glue will work for the others. You could even go more contemporary and use beads, buttons, etc...

*Use a gold paint pen to write inspirational sayings or quotes along lampshade edges, over archways, or along furniture molding. Try writing the names of all your family members along the edge of your dining table. You could either indicate place settings, or simply repeat the names over and over again, all the way around.

*Make a nature wreath or tower out of all those collected nature items! Glue moss to a grapevine wreath, then add the items you love...driftwood, pine cones, acorns, bird nest, seed pods, dried flowers, etc... To make an impressive centerpiece, cover a small tomato cage with chicken wire and moss. Then use floral wire and hot glue to build your own nature tower!

*Make lampshade covers out of fabric, or here's a great way to make one out of pleated paper! Pleat fold a piece of heavy paper large enough to cover the lampshade. Try decorative cardstock, or leftover wallpaper. You might even be able to get wallpaper scraps from your local wall-covering store just for the asking! Use a paper punch and punch holes evenly spaced along the top edge, and down the seam.

Now use a pretty coordinating ribbon to lace through the holes, and tie at the bottom. As always when working with light fixtures, be careful of your cover touching any heat source. Now either slip it over an existing lampshade, or tie it to the wire skeleton of an old one. (Use your punch and a little more ribbon, be sure to trim the ribbon on the inside so it doesn't touch the bulb.)

*Want no-sew pillow covers, perhaps for the change of seasons? Try one of these!

1. Lay a pillow form sandwiched between two cloth napkins, and tie at the four corners with pretty ribbon.
2. Lay a pillow on a large piece of fabric diagonally, then fold in opposing corners, tying the last two corners together to hold the cover in place.
3. Roll an old bath towel into a neckroll/bolster shape, then roll a piece of fabric around it, and tie at each end.

Hint: If you want to finish the edges, get some fusible hem tape and use your iron!

*Use one of the new paints for ceramics and glass to stencil your tile backsplash and give it a custom new look! If you don't want to paint, there are also new rub-on transfers for tile available at craft stores. This is also an option for dressing up your dinnerware. Create one of a kind place setting with the same simple stencil, stamp or sponge techniques touted elsewhere in this book. Just be sure to use glass paint designed for eating ware. If you can pick up some clear dishware at a great price (import stores are a great supplier) you can paint on the underside of the dish, and the designs will last much better. Try this technique for creating that holiday dinnerware you never splurged on!

*Use a small square sponge to sponge a checkerboard pattern on furniture-simply alternate the squares in each row. This works great as a wall border, too. You can make it as deep or as narrow as you wish, or try adding more than one color to the pattern.

*If you happen to have a table with a recessed glass top, try inserting memorabilia under the glass. Photos, greeting cards, programs, or your grandmothers' old love letters would all make great personal touches.

Ok, now that we've got your creative juices flowing, it's your turn! Look around your rooms and decide where you need a fresh accessory the most...wall art, a tablescape, a boring piece of furniture? Pick your favorite ideas, consider the style of your room, and start personalizing your home.

I hope you are starting to think of decorating in a new light. Finish one project that you're proud of, that you know you saved tons of money on, and I think you will be hooked. (And your home will be gorgeous, and more importantly, clever and personal.) Just remember, it's all a work in progress, especially when your on a tight budget...you don't have to do everything, right now.

Notes

Notes

Chapter Four

Kid's Rooms

Nowhere in decorating your home will you be able to have more fun with creativity than in your kid's rooms. You can let your imagination fly, do outrageous projects, wild colors, or fantasy dream rooms.

Rule # 1: There aren't any! Ok, there is one. Safety. As a parent my children are the most treasured things in my life …please use your common sense with any project, take in the age, ability and personality of your child, and make sure the room is above all a safe place for him/her to explore life. If in doubt, consult professionals, or go to www.safechild.net for great info on all things related to child safety. In fact, every parent should go there anyway!

Large objects must be secured to wall studs, don't use any fabrics or cords they can get tangled up in, check your blinds for cords that can choke a young child, and use socket plugs in every outlet.

Decorating children's rooms is much like any other room…the best first step is to choose a theme. Again, it can be as simple as their favorite colors, but this is your chance to give your child that dream room…total fantasy, one meant to spark the mind and imagination. By the way, I want to mention that I feel this is very important in this day and age of video addicted children…kid's tend to forget how to use their own creative minds.

Preschoolers are all about learning, but they do most of their learning through play and imagination. I think it's important to provide environments that support that imagination play, and allow them to be creative. While most of us are aware of the academic introduction to children this age in letters and numbers, kids also need to be able to explore with their imaginations in every way possible.

There are many ways to provide an environment to foster children's exploration, and it doesn't require lots of money. Their academic learning can be stimulated by providing lots of books, freely available in their space, or something as simple as sponging letters, words and numbers on their walls with paint. Providing small chalkboards or dry erase boards are a great way to get kids to experiment with spelling, or you can buy chalkboard paint and turn a whole wall into a learning experience quite inexpensively.

Imagination should take equal priority in a child's room, because it is through play a child learns the most. Find out what your child is really interested in, and then turn it into a theme for the room. This could be something as simple as their favorite colors, or as elaborate as a princess kingdom complete with throne headboard and muraled walls. Forget fear of decorating and let your child's enthusiasm give you confidence. They are NOT art critics! There is so much you can do with a little imagination and inexpensive materials. Allow for functional pieces in the room, including a place for them to draw and read. Provide a box full of clothing for them to play dress up and explore roles, blocks for them to build fanciful structures (you can make wooden blocks quite simply and cheaply with 2x4's, a good saw, and some sandpaper), and again, plenty of books. Get a library card for your child, encourage them to draw pictures of the books they read, and hang those pictures proudly in their rooms. Give them something to care for, be it a fish, a plant, or a treasure from the family. (Make sure you supervise this "caretaking", and concentrate on the successes, not the failures!)

Children must be included in decorating your own rooms, because as they are trying to foster their own independence, even at this young age, they will appreciate and enjoy much more something they had a part in creating. Allow them to talk about what they would want in their rooms, and then help them to come up with a drawing you can both agree is possible. Don't make the drawing too detailed, as children at this age take things more literally than we do, and you might find a very upset 4 year old who doesn't understand why the drawing has toys on all the shelves that he doesn't own! ("So, when are we going to the toy store, Mom?" is NOT what you want to hear!)

Provide storage space in other rooms of the house for them to keep their own towels, toothbrushes, and bubble bath. Keep stools available to make it easy for them to foster some independence in daily care of themselves. Encourage their participation in the kitchen, but make sure to teach them to always have help from an adult. Review safety rules with them every time they cook. Keep pot handles turned in, and try to cook on the back burners. Keep knives in a latched drawer. Give them their very own stirring spoon. Let them help plan a menu. Teach them to set the table and use table manners.

47

It isn't necessary to turn every room of your house into a playground in order to provide a great place for your kids to learn to be their best!

Some ideas for great theme rooms? Well here's a list of idea starters.

Sports
Animals
Mountains/Forest
Farm
City
Princess/Knight
Shapes
Letters/numbers/words
School
Pirate/sailor
Jungle
Bugs
Favorite Characters, i.e. Mickey, Pooh, Blues Clues
Music Groups
Celestial
Garden
Ocean
Ballerina
Space

The steps to take are all the same...walls, windows, floors, furnishings and accessories.

Paint is always a big player in my kid's rooms, so if you are afraid of painting...get over it! You do not have to be an artist either...for the younger set, it is actually an advantage to paint kindergarten like images, because they are simple for the young eye, and they can better identify with them. Utilize coloring books to copy from, get on the internet to find images of your theme, print them on a color printer, and decoupage them straight on the wall. Look at your own kid's drawings to see how they see these images. It isn't difficult; all you need is confidence in yourself. The worst thing that can happen is that you don't like it. That's the neat thing about paint, you CAN paint again!

Try some of the new paints available for children's rooms...chalkboard paint is available in several colors, and allows you to create a large chalkboard, or an unusual shaped board for a fraction of what it would cost to buy a traditional board. Take advantage of the different colors to incorporate the board into your room design...turn a painted mountain into a chalkboard, or the post office of a town? Be sure to use several coats of the specialty paint, and prime the chalkboard before use by thoroughly coloring it with the side of a piece of chalk (not the end), then erase.

Also available now are magnetic paints. These paints can be used as a base coat for your regular paint. Again, use several coats. When your final painting is done and dry, your child will be able to use magnets on his wall! This is a great learning tool, provide them with magnetic numbers and letters you can find at any dollar shop, or buy sheets of magnetic material from your craft store or office supply store, and design your own.

I don't recommend wallpaper for kid's rooms...first, it's expensive. Second, it always peels in a high use room such as a kid's rooms. Third, it's expensive! There are so many easy ways to simulate wallpaper or borders with paint and stamps, sponges, stencils, or contact paper, and it's so much cheaper!!!

Ok, now it's time to use your imaginations...use the room themes above or the ideas below as a starting point, get your child involved, and be sure to choose a room theme that *they* would enjoy, not just one you think is cute.

Cheery Nursery

Do your kids love those self-stick character wall decorations, but you think Mickey Mouse just floating in the air doesn't quite cut it? A great way to integrate such wall décor is to create a mural type background for them to "live" in. It is easier than you think, anyone can do this!

Make a quick drawing of a simple scene, a favorite is a grassy area with a big tree, clouds, sun, flowers, etc Remember this is a child's room, you don't need to be an artist. Simple is the key, and these are all very simple shapes!

Paint the wall (or walls) a pastel background color, blue works great to indicate sky, but any pastel color will give the illusion; after all, the sky is not always blue! You don't have to do this treatment to all the walls; often one is sufficient to add great impact.

Use a pencil to lightly sketch in the larger areas, just to get a perspective. Try to have furniture in its final position, so that it will appear part of the scene.

Use either leftover latex paint, or acrylic craft paint, and go for it! Remember, the idea is to make it look like a child's drawing, so again, if you could paint in kindergarten, you can do this!

Remember to let one color dry before you paint with another, and thin the paint with water if necessary to make it flow smoothly. It may take a couple of coats on the larger areas.

You may want to outline or accent later with paint pens, or you can add more dimension and detail by cutting objects from colored adhesive tape or contact paper, and adding them to the scene. Some good ideas are apples for the tree, tulip or daisy flowers, leaves, fence posts (wood grain contact paper is great for this) etc..

The last step is to simply add your self-stick characters to the scene! Wait a day or two for the paint to dry really well first, and don't feel you have to use the characters at all, you may like the room on it's own!

Finally, if you can't paint because you're a renter, you can cut the tree from pieces of poster board, and stick to the wall with poster putty.

Cut the clouds out of white contact paper, and outline them with a black marker BEFORE you put them on the wall.

Simple flower shapes can be cut out of colored and printed contact, and stems and leaves can be made out of green adhesive tape. If you can't find colored tape, try markers, or call a teacher supply store for the bright primary contact paper.

Garden Bedroom on a Budget

My youngest daughter has a garden bedroom, and it's my favorite room in the house. More than once after a long day I've been found rocking in a chair in her room surrounded by sunny yellow walls, floating clouds, blooming flowers and happy butterflies. She's only 2, but I hope she likes it as much as I do!

Getting started is easy. Just picture the garden you dream about in your mind, simplify it, and make it happen! The first thing I always do is bring out the paints, and painting a garden on the walls is much easier than it sounds. Paint the wall a background color that matches your mood...blue, yellow, pink, light green, and lavender all evoke a garden light. First, consider stencils. You can find small ones with blossoms and leaves at craft stores for less than a buck, you can cluster the flowers for larger designs, and tape off any part of the stencil you don't like. Then simply paint stems freehand with a brush and slightly thinned paint. After it dries, you can add more depth to leaves and stems by highlighting a little with some off white paint, just touch a little line on the edges where the light would realistically hit, here and there.

Another way to add painted flowers is with stamps, again, just freehand the stems. I like to add some painted fencing; a wide foam brush with thinned paint makes a great rustic look. Again, because the foam brush gives you relatively straight edges, you can just freehand it. Foam brushes are very cheap at the crafts store. You could also mask off your fence, and even an arbor behind the bed!

I like to keep the flowers together in clusters, for example, a group of sunflowers, then a group of roses, then some hollyhocks. Of course, you can repeat the groups, but it looks more cohesive than sprinkling the different flowers through randomly.

For a 3-d effect, consider cutting blossoms from felt, layer several together, then push a colored tack through the center to hold it to the wall, and also be the center of the flower! You can also use the felt flower idea to sew flowers to a comforter, curtains, or even dress up their furniture with a glue gun! When sewing, use leftover buttons as the centers. Felt is cheap, and you can use scraps!

If you are really ambitious, paint the ceiling blue and rag some clouds on with an old rag and some craft paint.

Finally, add some garden accessories...terra cotta pots for dresser top storage, a piece of lattice as a display board, make some simple wood planters for bookshelves, let your imagination travel to the outdoors!

Princess Bedroom

I think all my girls at one point have wanted a room that makes them feel like a princess. Well, here's one that REALLY will!

I think the focus of a princess room should be the bed, as in a bedroom it is the equivalent to a throne. You want to invoke the feeling of luxury without spending a lot of bucks, so here are my suggestions on what to concentrate on to get that "princess" environment just right!

Paint. Paint the entire room a beautiful rich color. Rich colors are key here whether they are for paint or fabric. Make a simple stencil from sturdy thin cardboard of a swag, and stencil it over and over around the room at ceiling line in a rich accent color. Try using a gold metallic paint marker to accent around the room. If you are brave, try painting one wall as if it was a wall of her castle, with a window looking out at the forest or clouds in the sky. Keep it simple; it doesn't have to be elaborate.

Fabric. If her bedspread just isn't the right colors, make one! Use sheets for cheap precut fabric and line it with an old blanket from your linen closet or a garage sale. It doesn't have to be fancy, just rich in color. Make a pillow cover for her with details like buttons, lace, and appliqués from scrap satin or other luxe type fabric. The trick is to make the majority of the fabric projects from cheap cotton material, maybe even the same sheets as the bedspread, then add small bits of the expensive fabrics to give the illusion of luxury. Add throw pillows to the bed, and layer fabrics. Check your linens for lacy cloth napkins, pieces of a velour towel that were torn or stained, etc for quick cheap items to make pillows with. Add details like buttons or ribbon bows. Add a folded quilt at the foot; use a sheet for a bedskirt (thrift stores!) throw fabric over a dressing table.

Make an incredible fantasy headboard. Ok, I know you're thinking there is no way to do this without spending a couple hundred bucks. Wrong! Imagination goes so far, and isn't that the reason we want to create a fantasy room to begin with? Choose a shape for your headboard, I like a crown. A castle would be a good choice also. Now choose your material according to your budget. If you or someone you know has a jigsaw, you could cut out a large crown from plywood. Remember to make it large in scale to make impact behind the bed. Check with a contractor of a local building site...they have many large scraps of wood siding they may let you have for free! If that isn't possible, all is not lost! Craft stores sell a product called foam core board, which is kind of like two layers of poster board sandwiched between layers of foam for stability. It is easily cut with a craft or utility knife. After you cut out your crown, (and remember scale is key, the bigger the better) simply either paint it or cover it with rich looking fabric and a glue gun. You want it to contrast from the wall so it will stand out as the focal point in the room. Now use your glue gun to add embellishments...small jewels from garage sale jewelry, sparkly beads, buttons, and tassels made from string or embroidery floss, etc. It might be best to gather all your materials and preplan your placement before you start gluing. Now attach it to the wall with nails, Velcro, or screws into studs if you use wood. Don't feel it has to start at the floor, position it behind the bed in whatever spot it gives the best impact, remember you are attaching it to the wall, not the bed.

If all else fails, you could even directly paint the crown on the wall right behind where the bed will be using left over craft paints...simply add the same embellishments to the wall once the paint is dry to give it a dimensional effect.

If you use your budget skills and look for materials around you...garage sales, thrift and dollar stores, clearance centers, building sites, etc, you can accomplish an incredible room for your little princess on very little money. Don't be afraid to employ the help of a friend or neighbor, or to try out an idea you have! Good luck and be brave!!!

Camper's Room

My 3 year old loves the outdoors. So when we moved to a new house and he finally got his own room, I decided what better than to let him enjoy the great outdoors all the time! Here are some great ideas for a budget bedroom for your great outdoorsman (or woman!)

Paint the walls a pale green to give the illusion of forest light. Trace a few evergreen trees (or whatever type your child would identify with) on the walls with pencil. Its easy, just a few simple shapes make up a tree! Remember kindergarten! Paint in the trees with common craft paint, or leftover house paint. Think about picking up one of those pop up playhouses as a tent…this actually inspired this whole idea for me. My son got one for Christmas, it was too big for our small family room, and so I put it up OVER his toddler bed! Instant tent, and instant home sweet home for him. You could also make a faux tent out of a sheet and a few dowels attached to the wall behind the bed. Just pull back the fabric from the dowels like the open door to a tent would be. Now pencil in a few simple logs in the corner for a campfire. (Yes, now you must paint them, this is easy!) You could also nail or glue cut dowels or branches to simulate logs, this would also give it depth. If your child has room, pick up a sturdy camp chair at a yard sale and make a comfy place to roast imaginary marshmallows. On your curtains, or the closed side of your mini blinds, sponge paint a deep blue, and add a few bright yellow stars for when the sun goes down. If you want to get really dynamic and dimensional, you could attach a large branch to the wall in the corner to imitate a real tree. The only thing that's left is a few hotdogs and s'more makings, and you've got an eternal camping trip! All for a couple dollars worth of paint, and a little scrap fabric for tent makings!

Ocean Room

I think the bedroom I hear kids ask for most often is an ocean fantasy bedroom. It also happens to be one of the easiest, with some of the greatest fantasy quotient for the kids! Don't be afraid of a little painting, and even *you* are going to love it!

Paint the walls a great ocean color as a base; it doesn't necessarily have to be an azure blue! If you love to experiment, try dividing the wall into horizontal thirds, and use a slightly different shade for each section-darkest on the bottom, lightest near the ceiling. You can use a brush dipped in water to blend the colors into each other before the paint dries. This can also be carried onto closet doors, to make the whole room seem really there.

Get yourself some good coloring books with pictures of the type of fish and sea life you would like to see on the wall. Remember, you don't have to have all the details or colors; it's just to give you a guide. Trace some simple fish, coral, and starfish onto the walls, and don't forget to add some bubbles. Try to take into account where the furniture will be placed when you're done, you don't want your best fish half hidden behind the dresser! Some people have actually borrowed projectors, and projected the image onto the wall for tracing.

Now it's just a matter of a little bright craft paint, maybe a paint pen for some details, and the best part of the room is almost done! You don't have to match the pictures exactly, just use whatever leftover paint you have and save money. Keep in mind that some colors may require a couple of coats.

Finally, the details! Bright tropical colors for the bedding and curtains seems to work great, but if it all is getting to be a bit much to your eye, tone it down by using naturals in the fabric, such as a gauzy material blowing in the breeze at the windows, and an earth toned comforter as your sail. Sew up some simple stuffed throw pillows for the bed in great sea shapes such as a starfish or a whale. Glue found seashells and driftwood to the bottom edge of the lampshade and to the curtain tiebacks. A hot glue gun is great for this! Speaking of curtain tiebacks, this is a great place to use that rustic rope from the basement, or pick some up cheap at the local home improvement store. A sailboat headboard can be made (or painted) with just a dowel or piece of molding as the mast, then two large triangles of hemmed fabric, one slightly shorter and smaller then the other. Small pennant flags can be made to run dome the mast, to show all the marvelous places the adventurer has visited. Good luck, and let us hear how those great rooms turn out!

Ballerina Room

There are so many little ballerinas out there, and some not so little! I have tried to come up with some ideas to offer you more than just ballerina wallpaper and pink everything!

Use traditional ballerina colors in your fabrics, and a very understated color on the walls. This way the little girl won't outgrow the room quite as fast, and it will be easier to change over to a new theme without having to repaint! Try using sheers, and tulle types of fabrics at the windows for texture and "feel". They also happen to be very cheap!

Buy cheap closet door type mirrors at your home improvement center and install several of them on the wall, studio style. If you choose, you could even use closet doweling and some brackets to set up a "barre". Just be sure to secure the brackets well in the wall studs!

There are many greeting cards etc... now that feature toe shoes, ballerinas, etc... and are quite nice photographs. Frame them up as artwork for the room, or frame some performance music, perhaps from their last recital?

Instead of cutesy wallpaper border, find a toe shoe stamp and design your own wall design. There are stencils too, but be careful with older kids... the ribbony, frilly type usually available can appear too "babyish" to them. Also consider stamping a key piece of furniture, or even the window treatments.

Try expanding from the usual pink into blues and purples also, to give the room a more unique appearance.

Remember, you can make her feel like a real "grown up" prima ballerina in her own room!

Space Room

My 8 year old daughter Kayla just happened to be studying the solar system this week, and sparked my imagination into a space bedroom, so if you have a budding astronaut at your house, this is for you!

Like many of my projects, first off is paint. Paint the entire room, including the ceiling, a deep blue. Sponge some stars all over the walls and ceiling with glow in the dark paint, which you can get at any craft store. You'll get the best effect if you vary the size of the stars, and don't try to space them evenly, nothing in nature is symmetrical. You can either buy pre cut star sponges from the craft store, cut your own stars from a household sponge, or you can get compressed cellulose sponge from the craft store for a more precise star. The compressed sponge comes flat like cardboard, you cut it into the shape you desire, then soak it in water and it magically expands. My kids fight over who gets to perform the magic!

Get colored poster board to cut out your planets, and hang from the ceiling with a tack and thread. You could use Styrofoam balls, but I find them hard to color, and too heavy for a tack. A great little touch to the poster board planets would be to get a glow in the dark marker and outline the craters, land mass, eye in Jupiter, etc. A great web resource to research you solar system is www.spacekids.com.

A blue or yellow comforter cover can be made out of two sheets sewn together and left open at one end to insert the old comforter. Shaped pillows made out of scrap fabric or felt are a great detail, star, moon, sun, etc

For window covering, you could have something as simple as dark blue curtains to match the walls, to a roller shade customized to match the walls when its closed. How would you do that? You can buy adhesive backed roller shades at the craft store-you cut a piece of dark blue material to fit, press it to the adhesive, then stamp with glow in the dark stars to match the walls. You could also stamp the curtains with the stars...be sure the paint is meant for fabric, and heat set it for 20 minutes in the dryer if you plan on washing it.

If you happen to have a woodworker in the house, or have access to a jigsaw, you could make a headboard in a simple space shape out of plywood or scrap wood, how about a rocket? At least ½ inch is necessary; if it's large, try ¾ inch wood. Remember, safety is a number 1 priority in a child's room, so use your common sense. Bolt it to the wall if necessary to keep it from accidentally falling on a child. Paint with craft paint or leftover house paint, and sandwich between the wall and the bed. You could also use foam core board, and cut it with a sharp utility knife.

As for accessories, pick up those gold stars teachers use from your local dollar store, and use them to dress up the room with detail. Gold paint pens can be used on furniture to add the glitter, use your imagination, and get your child involved, you'd be surprised how innovative they can be!

When you are decorating for children, remember that you are decorating for them, not for yourself. You may not like that particular shade of purple they chose for their room, but if it really delights the child, consider using it anyway. I always wanted to turn one of my kid's rooms into an ocean wonderland, but none of them were ever interested in it. But, even though I didn't get my waterworld, I have gotten great pleasure from watching my children learn and grow in environments that were right for THEM. Above all, enjoy your children and this time with them, as all too quickly, you will be teaching them to drive a car and helping them pick their college!

Kathleen Wilson

Notes

Notes

Chapter Five

Windows

*First things first- You CAN make your own curtains! If you have a sewing machine, great, but if not, all you need are an iron and some fusible hem tape, which you can get at any fabric or craft store.

*Use sheets for window covering material. Priced per yard, it is much less expensive than fabric off the bolt, and it doesn't require as much piecing because of the wide widths! Watch white sales, twin flat sheets seem to fit most windows with the least sewing, unless you are doing a sliding door, or something larger. Also check garage sales and thrift stores for flat sheets without mates.

*Dress up existing curtains by adding simple embellishments with either hot glue, or if you are going to be washing it, sewing it on. Add simple cording or fringe; try watching garage sales and thrift stores for fringe off old bedspreads and curtains. Add ribbon either to the bottom, top, or as edging. Turn rod pocket curtains into tab top by simply sewing on fabric strips or ribbon to the top, equally space. Sew on old beads or buttons, or make appliqué shapes to satin stitch or fuse onto the window treatment.

*If you have extra white sheets you'd like to press into service for windows, but they aren't the right color, just dye them! It can be easily done in your washing machine, just follow the manufacturers instructions. Or add pattern with paint. Fabric can be stenciled, stamped, or sponged with acrylic craft paint, and then heat set in the drier for 20 minutes. (Wait for the paint to dry to the touch, first!)

*You can make faux decorative shutters for your windows out of cardboard! Simply cover the cardboard with fabric and ribbon, and use ribbon to act as "hinges".

*Make the stained glass look cheaply and easily by covering your window with colored tissue paper. Simply wet the tissue with liquid starch, and apply in any pattern you choose. It will wash off later if you change your mind. Or paint directly on your window glass with water-based paint…add a few drops of liquid dish detergent and the paint will come off easily later with window cleaner.

*Lighten up winter windows by tacking a lace tablecloth inside the window frame, and leave the heavier drapes pulled back. Or, take the heavy drapes down altogether, and drape the lace right over the curtain rod.

*Use creative materials for tiebacks. How about old jewelry, strings of beads, small grapevine wreaths, (about 20 cents at the craft store) silk vining plants, rustic rope, chain, etc...

*Create an upholstered look cornice topper with cardboard! Cut heavy duty cardboard to the size you wish your finished window topper to be, and score it where you wish it to bend at the edge of the window. Cover it with batting (an old blanket or towel will do also) and your fabric, and staple or hot glue onto the backside. Be sure to use staples that are not so long they will poke out the front of the cornice! Use hot glue to add any trim, buttons, etc... and hang on the wall over the window with L-type brackets.

Be sure to be aware of how much of the back of your topper shows to the outside of the house when you hang it. You can also hang panels underneath the topper for a layered look. You wouldn't even necessarily need a rod, you could just shirr and staple them in place if you don't need them to draw, and the topper will cover the stapling.

*Another use for cardboard cornices? Instead of covering them in fabric, cover them with things that express the design of the room. For a child's room, glue on felt or craft foam cutouts, or try gluing on a collage of personal items. A collection of postcards, coloring book covers, personal art, etc... More adult rooms might benefit from natural items, such as pine cones, pressed leaves, etc. for a nature inspired room, playing cards for a rec room, labels for a kitchen, use your imagination!

*While we're still on the subject of cardboard cornices, try using them in unusual shapes to add architecture to the window. Arched at the top, scalloped at the bottom, use those simple details to make a difference in your rooms. Try carrying the arch all the way to the ceiling to add height and drama. After all, we're just talking a little more cardboard! If you have a larger window you'd like to try this with, ask an appliance store to save you a box from a refrigerator. By the way, you could also use foam core board from the craft store, but why, when cardboard is free?

*Want to make those fabulous rosette window treatments, but don't want to pay for those expensive "frames"? Use plastic six-pack holders to pull your fabric through, and make those great rosettes for free! You can cut them down to one or two openings, or use several together to create more extravagant treatments. You can also use twist ties to secure you individual rosettes. The plastic will also double over itself similar to a rubber band if the fabric is thin. Why not use rubber bands, you ask? They tend to leave marks on the fabric, and they are so tight they make it hard to make adjustments.

*Hang ornamental items from your rod for interest. Sun catchers are one of the more obvious choices, but how about small birdhouses, strings of beads, interesting (perhaps antique) utensils, glass ball ornaments, or even small bunches of fresh or dried flowers!

*Use inexpensive muslin to drape over and around a curtain rod for a great "airy" romantic treatment. Wash and dry the muslin first to get a great "wrinkled" texture, and work with the draping until you find an arrangement that works for you. This is especially nice in rooms with natural themes.

*Who says you have to have window treatments at all? If you have nice looking rods, try removing your curtains in the summer and replacing them with dried flowers, or drape it with a silk vine.

*Use a favorite old quilt on your window. This is great for a "country" look.

*Make a room look lighter and larger by hanging the window treatments clear of the window itself, but just leave the edge covered, it lets in the most light, and gives the illusion there is more window behind the covering material.

*Hang swags of fabric instead of valances- no expensive rod to buy, and you can use irregular pieces of leftover fabric. You can even use tape instead of sewing- who's gonna see it?

*Use simple fabric roller shades, then paint, stamp, or stencil them so they will co-ordinate with the room when closed.

*Close mini blinds and then sponge on stars or simple shapes; they will show when the blinds are closed at night, and warm up the space! Or you can apply shapes using contact paper, or those coordinated vinyl appliqués meant for walls. (You know the ones; they have your kid's favorite cartoon characters on them?) You have to take the blind off the window to apply. Simply lay the blinds down on a flat surface with the slats in the closed position. Press the appliqué or contact paper to the back of the slats. And simply use a sharp razor blade or utility knife to cut the appliqué between the slats. Now rehang the shade, and whenever you close the blinds at night, you will not feel like you have a blank hole in the wall!

*Another option to dress up shades involves roller blinds. Roller blinds are fairly inexpensive, but definitely rate in the boring category! You can fuse fabric onto the blinds as long as they are made of a material that won't easily melt. Use fusible webbing available at the craft store, and cut a piece of fabric the same size as the shade. After applying the webbing to the wrong side of the fabric (follow manufacturer's instructions) peel off the paper backing, center on the shade, and fuse with a low iron heat. Experiment with the iron temperature until you get the adhesion you want, without melting the shade. Also available from the craft store are blinds with an adhesive side to make this process easier.

*Make a valance out of simple shapes cut from colored poster board or foamy sheets you can get at the craft store, and glue to the wall along the upper edge of the window, or to a rod itself.

*Use cloth napkins or placemats as a valance; just lay them on the rod diagonally, slightly overlapping. This is a great way to use doilies or vintage linens as well.

*Use a stencil and some frosted glass paint found at the craft store to add delicate details to the edges of your windows for a custom look for very little money.

*Try to think out of the ordinary when it comes to curtain rods. Not only will it add interest and personality, it could help cut the cost dramatically! Tour your local home improvement store for ideas... pipes, PVC, closet doweling, etc. Anything can be painted, wrapped with sleeves of fabric, or hid under a valance. Other options include large branches or sapling tree cuttings, paddles or oars, yardsticks, ski poles, etc. Use your creativity, and look towards your room's theme for inspiration! How about cup hooks with tab curtains hanging from them? You can hang these either from the wall or the ceiling to give the room more height and scale, and draw them back with tiebacks if necessary. This is great for hanging sheers from a window to get some privacy, but keep the window light.

*Another option for hanging window treatments inexpensively is to use lathing strips. Lathing strips are narrow lightweight wooden boards that can be found at any home improvement store for pennies.

Simply cut it to the size you wish your window treatment to be, and staple the fabric to the back of the lathing strip. You can either staple it flat, or pleat and gather it as you go for a fuller, softer look. Now simply nail the strip in place from the underside. The fabric will flow over the strip and hide the nails.

*Use a floor screen as a window treatment. It is easily changed, can be used in other parts of the room during the day, and offers privacy.

Notes

Notes

Chapter Six

Outdoor Rooms

Many times when the weather becomes sultry, the only place we want to be is in our favorite chair on the porch, sipping ice-cold lemonade! So, if we are to spend our summer months languishing with Mother Nature, why not treat our "outdoor room" to a little freshening up, and make our time outdoors more enjoyable! Here are some great, easy ideas you can use to add your own personal style to a much used "summer home"!

*Treat your outdoor space just like an indoor room when you think about decorating it. Mother Nature has got the ceiling covered in most cases, but you should think about floors, furniture, accessories, color, and, yes, walls, just like any other project. Choose a theme, even if it's just color!

*Use existing fencing, tall plants, trellising, etc... for your walls, or just imply that walls exist by arranging your furnishings as if they did.

*Dress up old patio furniture with cushions (easily made out of leftover fabric), a little paint, and maybe some stenciling or stamping. Detail brings that "home" feeling to the space. If you don't have furniture, buy those inexpensive resin chairs and make cushions out of a bright cheery fabric.

*Tables can be made out of a lot of "junk." Stepladders make great little drink tables. I found one of those large "spools" used by the utility companies in my yard when I moved in - it's a bit weathered, but turned on its side, it makes a terrific table. Paint leftover squares of plywood and set them on top of unused large pots, or on a birdbath. Two pots and a larger piece of wood make a great coffee/breakfast table.

*Tiki torches are relatively inexpensive, and add great ambience! Forget that expensive outdoor lighting set!

*Make luminaries out of recycled cans to light a walkway. Remove labels, fill with water, and then put in the freezer for a couple of hours. When they're frozen, use a hammer and nail to poke holes in a pattern, similar to punched tin. Stars, hearts, butterflies, even just

67

zigzag lines will let the light shine through in an interesting pattern. (The freezing of water prevents the can from denting when you punch it.) Thaw, drain, put some sand or gravel in the bottom to anchor a votive candle - instant charm, for the price of the candles. This is great for a party or barbecue, by the way!

*Paint those boring planters! Once again, a few tubes of craft paint and a little imagination can make all the difference. Nothing fancy is needed- stripes, dots, squiggles; sponged-on shapes all can make designer accents. How about gluing on some stones or shells?

*Since we are already painting planters, how about free ones? I recycle kitty litter buckets, plastic ice cream buckets, coffee cans, etc... Just poke some drainage holes in the bottom, paint and decorate, and plant!

Another option is to use a relatively new product called Flex-All. It is similar to a joint compound for the wall and can be found at most hardware stores or home improvement centers. Apply it to your surface like mud, I prefer to use my hands (wear gloves), or you can use a trowel. The idea here is to make the planter look like expensive stone or concrete. You can smooth it a bit with water, if necessary. Be sure to carry it at least several inches down into the interior of the pot so it will look authentic. Let dry as suggested by the manufacturer. Now you can either paint it to give it an aged look, or simply seal it with water based polyurethane. If you choose to paint, try some subtle techniques such as sponging or stippling in earth tone colors. Be sure, as always, that there are drainage holes in the bottom of the pot before you start this project!

Notes

Kathleen Wilson

Notes

Chapter Seven

Holiday Decorating

Let me say this is my favorite reason to decorate. Here you will find great ideas for the holidays, all of them easy on the pocketbook, and some of them are free! Have a wonderful holiday, and remember to stop every day to "smell the roses"!

*For a beautiful outdoor wreath (or indoor) without spending a fortune on craft supplies, try to remember you need not cover the wreath with decoration to make it special. Try just a few craft store "picks" in one corner, with a big bow. Or get some wire star garland (.69 cents at my store) and just wrap it loosely around the wreath. Hot glue some found pinecones to a corner, or try some old wooden ornaments. You also don't necessarily need to buy an expensive evergreen wreath to decorate, and inexpensive grapevine or straw wreath can be dressed up as well.

*Spray paint clay pots and saucers a metallic gold for sparkling coasters and utensil or candleholders for the season.

*If you have extra lights after stringing the tree, wind some through your potted plants for a special way to bring the sparkle throughout the room.

*For a simple but beautiful centerpiece, set three or five candles of different heights in the middle of the table on a tray, and then surround the bases of the candles with seasonal items. Low cost ideas? Cuttings from your Christmas tree, or from evergreen trimmings in your yard are a great first layer. Then how about shiny apples, glass ornaments turned hanger side down, found pinecones, nuts, wire star garland, leftover ribbon... By the way, the same idea can be used for Thanksgiving, just substitute fall leaves, squashes, mini pumpkins, etc...

*Buy those bags of cranberries when they go on sale for $1, and fill bowls that hold pillar candles, or fill a simple glass of water with them to just a few inches below the top, and put a floating candle in. Nuts can work the same way, but they tend to be more expensive. However, if you have a nut tree in your yard...

71

*Hollow out the center of an apple as a candleholder, and tuck a few tiny greens in between the candle and the apple. Just be sure the flame never comes near the twigs. A little lemon juice sprinkled on the cut part of the apple will help keep it from browning as much.

*Have a lot of scrap Christmas fabric from years past? Use it to make a simple square patchwork quilt as a throw for the couch, and add a lot of holiday spirit to the room! (Hint: use old blankets as batting- if you don't have any, check your thrift stores. Just be sure to wash in hot water, and dry at least 20 minutes in your dryer. White flat twin sheets on sale make great backing fabric.)

*Cut two of a simple holiday shape from felt, then sew or fuse them together, decorate with permanent markers or fabric paint (if you wish), and hang all over the house! Some very simple shapes could include stars, packages (glue or paint on some ribbon), mittens, snowmen, boots, Christmas trees, stockings, candy canes, gingerbread men (trace them from your cookie cutters) and the list goes on! If you have a rustic theme this year, it's not necessary to embellish them at all!

*Place a few inexpensive glass balls in a bowl and embellish with a few sprigs of greenery or some leftover ribbon. If you don't have an extra bowl (it is the holidays, after all!) try decoupaging a box with leftover Christmas wrap, or cover with a little fabric and glue.

*Take down your wall pictures and wrap them like a gift, then hang them back on the wall for great holiday cheer! You don't have to do this all around the house, how about just in the entry, or maybe the dining room?

*Place votive or pillar candles on a small mirror used as a tray. Tie sprigs of greens or cinnamon sticks on the candles with ribbon or raffia. Be sure the flame is far enough away from the embellishments!

*Make paper trees out of a square of pretty paper; preferably use a paper that is a little stiff. Simply roll the paper into a cone, and glue the edge with a hot glue gun. Perhaps some gold glitter or squiggles of paint to dress them up, and they will be beautiful on your mantel or as a centerpiece with greens. Try experimenting with different colors and textures...this would be a great place to use leftover cardstock or handmade paper! You could also do this with a piece of stiffened fabric.

*Tie greens or ornaments to the chandelier with a little Christmas ribbon; just make sure they don't hang low enough for any candles on the table to catch them on fire.

Above all, be creative, and have a wonderful holiday with those you care about!

Kathleen Wilson

Notes

Notes

Chapter Eight

Favorite Projects

Easy Slipcovers

One of the most expensive items in our rooms is our furniture, and we can't always afford to just replace it when it gets worn, outdated, or just no longer works in your room. However, custom slipcovers are very expensive, and elaborate slipcovers aren't that easy to make yourself. Here are instructions for some simple, casual covers that almost anyone can do.

First of all, use sheets instead of pieced fabric; it is MUCH easier and cheaper!

Measure your furniture, and buy a sheet size that will cover your furniture piece without it's cushions, tucked in and around the arms.

Use decorative cording if you like to tie around the "skirt" area to give it a more structured look. Simply tuck ends under the couch or chair. (You could even tape or staple the ends to the bottom of the piece, if you wanted.)

Now take each of your cushions and look at it as if you are wrapping a gift. Cut a piece large enough for your cushion, wrap it like a present, and safety pin it to the underside of the cushion. (Who's gonna see it?)

Add a few pillows and a throw, and you have changed the entire look of your furniture for little money, the covers are washable, and you can make one for each season if you want.

Remember to use what you learned in Creative Material Sources here. Sheets, blankets, and quilts can all be used for this project, and can be found at garage sales, thrift stores, and maybe even your own linen closet. Try wrapping the cushions with another, different fabric from the room. Remember, this is all about casual style, and slipcovers are definitely stylish!

Nature Wreaths and Crafts

Nature Wreaths: This is perhaps the easiest and most popular of the nature crafts! You can use any number of collected items for these, and you can add household objects too, you are only limited by your imagination!

First, you need a base. The easiest solution is to buy a grapevine (or straw, or Styrofoam) wreath at the craft store when the go on sale. They are very cheap, and are strong enough to hold up over the years. You can find them from just a few inches across, to a large 36 incher or more! You could also make your own by shaping a wire coat hanger, then wrapping it with fabric and batting scraps to make a firm base. Tie or glue the scraps on, a glue gun or floral wire is easiest if you are working alone. Just be sure you have enough objects to cover the whole wreath! (Or you might find you like the fabric scraps so much, you hang it on the wall and do what I do, buy a grapevine wreath!)

Next, choose your method of adhesive. Glue guns are my favorite, but you can use regular white glue if your items are lightweight. A hot melt glue gun will last longer and hold stronger, but remember, hot melt glue can damage Styrofoam and delicate materials, so in these cases, opt for the low melt gun. Other choices are floral wire, floral picks for straw wreaths, or even pieces of pretty ribbon to tie items on!

Design your wreath. I prefer informal, plan as you go type crafts, but that's me! If you need ideas, pick up a crafts magazine at the grocery store and thumb through, but just for ideas. You'll love it ten times more if it comes from inside you! Besides, if you don't like it, start over, most of the stuff was probably free! In general, related and larger items look better grouped, while smaller more like items look better in an all over design, but experiment!

Need ideas for natural items? Try some of these! Sea shells, small rocks and pebbles, acorns, seed pods, pressed leaves, dried flowers, wasp nests (no wasps, of course), bird nests, pretty dried grasses, driftwood, nuts, feathers, branches and twigs, mosses and lichens (be careful about collecting laws), whale baleen washed up on the beach, small animal skulls (ok, that one isn't for everyone!), barnacles on rocks, etc.. You get the idea here. If it holds beauty in your eyes, or

77

memories in your thoughts, turn it into something wonderful to warm and personalize your home!

You don't need to adhere to wreaths alone for this project, dress up any number of items with natural treasures. I glued pinecones and acorn caps onto a mirror frame, and it's now a unique and stunning focal point on my wall, for the cost of the hot glue! If you try this project and you get glue on the glass, simply wait for it to cool, and it will peel off easily.

Faux Fireplace

Ok, so Valentine's Day is around the corner, and you need a cozy fire to cuddle by? Or maybe, the winter chill has just reminded you how much you miss the basic element of fire to warm those long nights? Unfortunately, your home's builder wasn't the romantic you are, and you have no fireplace. Never fear, The Budget Decorator is here! Ok, so that's corny, but this project sure isn't!

The first thing to do is to determine what element you want your fireplace to be made of. A lot of this depends on the formality of your room, and the style of fireplace you choose to make. Paint, tiles, faux bricks, wood molding and plywood, scrap beadboard, it goes on as far as your creativity.

Next, you'll need to determine how much labor you want to put into the construction. The options range from a flat front "tromp loeil" style fireplace, to a wooden construction of an actual fireplace box and mantle.

Suggestions to get you started:

Faux stone fireplace

Mask off the entire area of the fireplace, and paint it a background color-this will be your grout color. Mask off an area that will be the firebox, paint it a matte black color. Take an ordinary household sponge and tear it into several different size irregular pieces, simulating pieces of rock or stone. In a paper plate, pour three earth tone colors of craft paint. Dab the sponge into the paint colors, don't worry about them mixing some, dab off the extra paint so it doesn't run, then "stamp"stones onto the fireplace background. Continue to alternate sponge sizes, leaving some space between stones for a natural masonry look. Alternatively, if you have access to many smaller stones, how about gluing the stones right to the painted background! Add a mantle; a simple pine shelf will do. Be sure to accessorize the mantle with personal photos, and most importantly, candles! Candles give the impression of fire, and the mantle and firebox complete the illusion. This would be a great choice for an informal rustic space.

Faux tile fireplace

Seen those cool contemporary ceramic or stone tiled fireplaces? Easy to do. Same concept as above, except slightly more formal. You could either mask off the tiles with ¼ inch masking tape and paint them, or if you can get some castoff tiles, you can glue on the real thing. I did mine with leftover faux marble self-stick tiles from a floor project, and plain white ceramic tiles are pretty cheap. Hint: If you use self-stick tiles, reinforce the adhesive with a glue gun! A flooring store might even have some discontinued tiles they would let you have for free.

Looseends.com sells paper mache stones and brick, although I don't find them particularly cheap, they are excellent quality, and might be worth it. Or, you could try your hand at making your own. Finish off the fireplace edge and firebox with some cheap wood molding, even lathing strip, and add a mantle!

Classic Faux Fireplace

For the labor-loving decorator, you could even construct an actual wood box, the most realistic of the choices! Since I don't pretend to be even a weekend woodworker, try the plans found on Internet sites or woodworking magazines..

So, now, I know what I'm doing on Valentines Day!

Paper Mache Accessories

OK, remember kindergarten? Save your newspapers and junk mail, and get ready for a great project for almost NO money!

Whenever I look for decorative vases and bowls, I almost always try this first.

Paper mache recipe 1

Add water to flour to make a thick paste. Adding a little salt will help repel molding. Dip strips of newspaper into the paste, thoroughly wetting them, then apply to your project. Allow to completely dry before painting. This recipe is good for large projects that require a lot of paper mache!

Paper Mache Recipe 2

Shred up newspapers into a large bowl or pot. Pour just enough boiling water over the paper to cover, allow to sit overnight. Shred and mash the newspaper in your hands to make a fine pulp. Add a few tablespoons of white household glue. This paste can be used almost as modeling clay, and is better suited to small projects with more detail.

Try combining the two. For instance, cover a foam wreath form to make a picture frame with recipe #1, but add details to the frame with the second recipe. The Second recipe can also be used over the first once it has dried to smooth and add more detail.

Mix up a batch of paper mache paste, and shred some newspapers. Find a mold for your item, a bowl or vase, anything you want to recreate that has an open shape. Remember those thrift stores! You will need to be able to slide the finished paper mache work off the item once its dry. Cover the item with a layer of foil to protect it and make removal possible.

Now simply apply several layers of paper mache over the item, allowing it to dry thoroughly between coats. Once you feel you've built it up enough to be strong enough to stand up on it's own, peel the paper mache off the item, taking the foil with it. Now you peel off the foil as best you can, use a utility knife to even out the edge if you wish, then prime and paint it, it's that simple! You can paint it everything from country quaint, to modern metallic, whatever fits in your scheme. Obviously, you don't want to put water in any of these vessels, but they are great for holding dried arrangements, or simply displayed on their own on a shelf or table. You could even accentuate them with a glue gun, and whatever fits…beads, coffee beans, etc…

I've also used paper mache and clean cardboard milk cartons to create decorative birdhouses…just cut out the opening with a craft knife after the final coat has dried. Then simply paint and decorate as you would any other!

Easy and Elegant Wall Finishes

The most economical way to treat your walls is without question, paint. There are so many choices out there with faux finishes, rich colors, and choices in texture and quality that it can be hard to decide where to start! Here we've included some great ideas for dressing your walls and making great impact in your rooms for very little money! Feel free to mix and match designs, and import the colors of your own rooms to create designer walls, for no more than a can or two of paint!

Wall 1: This is a simple faux finish wall that is simply sponged one color lighter over a base coat. Sponging is easy, and you don't have to buy an expensive sea sponge to do it! Just take a regular household sponge, and tear little bits away from the hard edges to give it a more natural and soft effect. Then simply dip your sponge into your paint, dab any excess off, and sponge over your base color! I don't recommend sponging over white unless you are looking for a cloud effect, you will get a much more subtle look from using two shades of the same color.

Wall 2: This treatment simulates expensive embossed wallpaper, and is great for a more formal room. Choose two shades of the same color, one lighter than the other. Paint the background the lighter color, and let dry thoroughly. Now use some painters tape to mask off vertical stripes similar to striped wallpaper, try making alternate stripes a different width. Lastly, brush a coat of clear polyurethane over every other stripe…when the light hits it, it will give the impression of elegantly textured wall covering!

Wall 3: This technique requires some painter's tape, and a stamp or a stencil to coordinate with your room. You can use many different combinations of stripes to simulate wall covering, chair rails, and borders. Use the stamp to enhance the design by following a border, using it as another wall covering for the upper half of a wall, or interspersed between the stripes..

Wall 4: This is a simple overall open pattern, most easily made with a stamp. One note about using stamps on walls, you only need a very small amount of paint, so be sure to blot it off, and do test prints. If you are working on a glossy surface and you make a mistake, you should be able to wipe it off quickly with a wet cloth. To guide you in placing your design straight down the wall, you can hang a string from a tack at ceiling line with a small weight attached to the free end, a bolt will do, or anything else you can tie to the end! I also recommend alternating the pattern each row. This idea works great over white walls to warm them up; you can use more than one color or stamp, but be sure they relate to each other and the room! For instance, a rose and a leaf might work well together in a garden room, but keep one stamp more dominant, either by using it more, or choosing a larger style than the other. This is also great for small rooms; especially on a white background because it gives the walls depth and helps them fade away a bit.

Easy Hook Rug

Great way to use all those fabric strips! Buy a piece of rug mesh at the craft store, very inexpensive. Using fabric strips and a hook of some kind (crochet hook works) reach through the top of the rug mesh with the hook, and pull the fabric strips up partially through each hole to form the loop of the rug. You may make the "pile" as deep as you like by simply pulling more or less through. When finished pulling fabric through all the holes, carefully turn it over and iron a piece of fusible webbing to the back of the rug to fit. This is like a giant sheet of glue that will hold the fabric in place. You may cut each loop to make a "cut pile" or leave the looped look.

You can be as creative as you like with this project...draw out a pattern on graph paper, or choose to do a random design. You could cut up old clothing, suits, sheeting, you name it. You could visit the thrift store for color combinations in your plan.

Salt Dough Embellishments

Sometimes my job is really cool, because every so often I get to pretend I'm in kindergarten again. This project is one of those times! I came up with this project as an inexpensive way to dress up wood molding…I was trying to make a grand entrance on the cheap, I love the carved wood appliqués I was seeing on high end furniture and cabinets, and the carved wood molding seen in very expensive rooms. However, even to buy those wood embellishments unfinished was WAYYYY expensive. So my solution? Salt dough, a little paint, and a glue gun!

Simply mix up a batch of salt dough with our recipe below. Roll it out on a floured board and cut it into the desired shapes. I used leaves and cut them freehand with a sharp knife, but you could use any simple shape, and you could even use cookie cutters if you want. Add details to your cutouts. I used my knife to add veins to my leaves, and pinched some of them together slightly to create a "ruffle" in the leaf. I wet my finger with water and smoothed out any rough edges, but you could sand them after they bake if you desire. Place them on foil or a cookie sheet. Bake them in a 250-degree oven for 1 hour, and then check them every 15 minutes until they are completely dry. (Check the bottom). After they cool, sand if needed, and then paint! I painted mine white, glazed them with a warm umber, then brushed them lightly with metallic gold craft paint and got a very elegant look. Now simply use your glue gun to adhere them to whatever needs dressing up… wood molding, shelf edging, cabinet doors, door frames, let your imagination guide you.

So, what we have here is a virtually free project that adds upscale class, elegant detail, and is a lot of fun in the process. On top of that, it's EASY!

Salt Dough Recipe

2 cups flour
½ cup salt

Water added by the tablespoon until the desired consistency
1-2 tablespoons salad oil added to help keep it from drying and cracking

Hint: Keep the dough you are not working with tightly covered until ready to use.

Candlescapes

Candles are all the rage right now, but whether you purchase them, or make your own they can be expensive. Here are some terrific ideas for making your candle displays demand attention, making them well worth it, and a better decorating value!

Cluster several candles on a shelf in front of a wall mirror, or use a small mirror as the candle tray. The mirror doubles the glow, therefore halving your candle budget!

Buy some floating candles for some great dinnertime candlescapes. (If you make candles, disposable tart pans make great molds.) Fill a plain water glass with fresh fruit, cover with water, and place a floating candle on top. Or simply float them in a pretty bowl for a simple centerpiece.

Place pillar candles in pretty bowls filled with greenery, nuts, fruit, or coffee beans. Try stacking two or more bowls for a tiered effect, perhaps tucking small flower sprig peaking out of the bottom bowl.

Use creative candleholders. Small terra cotta pots, special teacups, colorful bottles. Napkin rings seem to be the perfect size for votives, but be sure to protect the surface underneath.

Make your own candlesticks! Blocks of scrap 2x4 stacked and glued, then painted, make a great place for your pillars. How about old banister or headboard dowels, drilled to hold a taper? Even an old log chunk for a rustic or natural look.

Need a couple of hints on how to get the most from your candles? Place them in the refrigerator an hour before use, and they will burn longer. The first time you burn a candle, always burn it for one hour for each inch of diameter, and you will avoid the hole in the middle, wick disappearing trick! If you buy scented candles, always smell the bottom of the candle. If you only get a strong scent from the top, they have probably only been dipped in scent, and you will be disappointed. Finally, if your candles smoke, trim the wick to a quarter inch before burning. Have fun with candles, and be sure to check out candle making classes at your local craft shop!

Faux and Decorative Painting

Sponge painting

Sponge painting is great because it is easy, fast, requires little paint and materials, and did I mention it was easy? It can be used on walls, furniture, and accessories, and can give instant facelift to dull objects.

Don't let anyone convince you that you have to go buy an expensive sea sponge to do this. I've used plastic grocery bags, cloth diapers, even old clothing...(Ok, now it's called ragging, same technique, more subtle look.) But you can use a plain old kitchen sponge, and here's the secret....tear away all the hard edges of the sponge, even tear chunks from the center to give it an irregular appearance.

Now choose your paint, and sponge! Remember to sponge sparingly at first, you can always add more later. Also, dab the paint off on your plate first, you only need a little paint on the sponge, or it will be too gloppy. Practice first on a paper bag, and remember to change the direction of your hand occasionally, the idea is not to get a pattern going.

Try combining sponge painting with stenciling or decorative painting, tape off a border and use it just there, you can even sponge paint over glassware with the new glass paints available at your craft store.

Marbleizing

There is a very simple technique to marbleizing that is popular in the home decorating world today, and you won't believe how easy it is until you try it.

Simply choose two to four colors of paint within the same color scheme, one light, one medium, and one dark.

Using a regular paintbrush, dip the brush into all the colors. Now simply pounce the paintbrush over the surface to get a mottled effect. It might help to keep a picture of a piece of marble nearby to refer to. Use the different colors to add shading, or tone down an area you think is too bright.

When finished with the surface, take a small artists liner brush, dip it into either the lightest or darkest color you used, (thin with a little water, if necessary) and paint veins by dragging the brush over the surface, wiggling it as you go. Don't go overboard on the veining. Remember also to bring the veins over the edges for a realistic finish.

I think sealing it with a gloss clearcoat or polyurethane gives the most authentic look of polished marble.

Crackling

Crackling is very popular as aged finishes have become so much a part of showcasing warmth and history in our homes. It **can** be done without purchasing expensive crackling kits.

Crackled finishes are a simple chemical reaction. All you need are two colors of *latex* paint, one a base coat that will peek through, and one a top coat, that you will see the most of, and household glue. That's right, direct from your kid's art box.

Sand and prime your piece if necessary, then paint with your base coat. Remember, this will be the color the will just peek through, so it's best if it contrasts with the topcoat. Let dry.

Now mix household glue with equal parts water, and brush onto your base coat. This can be done easiest with a foam brush. Allow the glue to dry until just tacky, about 30 minutes.

Now for the reaction part. Brush on your topcoat directly over the glue coat. Don't brush over any one area more than once; you will ruin the crackle effect in that area. You should start seeing the crackling take place within a minute or so. The size of the crackles has a lot to do with your technique in applying the topcoat, so experiment a little first. Long, smooth strokes tend to produce larger more dramatic cracks than short strokes, and if you really want a subtle effect, try sponging or ragging on the final coat. Allow to dry overnight.

If you wish to further antique your work, simply dab or brush it with some wood stain, then wipe off. Repeat until you get the look desired.

You can seal with polyurethane or clearcoat, or coat it with common furniture wax.

Chapter Nine

Web Resources

There are a lot of great sites on the web, but fewer for those of us on a tight budget. If you aren't on the Internet yet, it's time to get there. Definitely a budget decorator's best friend! There are inexpensive Internet providers. Try www.juno.com, www.netzero.net, or www.attworldnet.net. If you don't have a computer, many libraries now offer free time on the Internet.

I have sectioned off the website information into three categories: Inspiration, Suppliers, and Instruction. Use the websites and catalogs for inspiration. You can gain ideas for themes, individual projects, or you may just find that one quality item that makes your room. Finally, I have provided information on the growing community of "Frugalites". That is, websites and newsletters where you can get more information on living on a tight budget.

Inspirational Sites: Use these sites with a critical eye. See something you think is exactly what you want? Try to figure a way to make the look, without breaking the bank. I hope the ideas in this book have just opened up your mind to new creativity!

www.thebudgetdecorator.com- *The* best place to get all your budget decorating ideas!

www.drexelheritage.com- Great inspiration for many styles of rooms and furnishings.

www.ballarddesigns.com- View what's hot in accessories and furnishings.

www.wisteria.com- More accessorizing inspiration.

www.kraftmaid.com- The best place on the web for planning your dream kitchen.Great ideas that can be interpreted into faux finishes, accessorizing, and embellishing with molding. Even patterns to paint your floors and counters!

www.countrycurtains.com- Good ideas for curtains to either make, or buy from them. Good company to do business with.

www.crateandbarrel.com- Good inspiration for just about everything, including kids rooms. Lot's of ideas that can be made at home. Some one of a kind things that might be worth the price!
www.calicocorners.com- Fabric supplier with ideas for anything you can sew or hang!
www.waverly.com- Fabrics, projects, great rooms to view.
www.wood-mode.com- Kitchen and furniture photo gallery.
www.homeportfolio.com- One of those sites with everything! Inspirational, and great planning tools.

Suppliers

www.renovatorssupply.com- Great source for hardware, amongst many other decorative items. Prices very reasonable.
www.hydrosil.com- Website for a new concept in heating your home at substantial savings.
www.surefit.com- Slipcovers By Mail…with ideas and photos.
www.abwf.com- The discount house for blinds and wallpaper.
www.linenspot.com- The only place online to look for linens and the like, this site is a directory for all the major linen suppliers online, from Kmart to Eddie Bauer Home. Outlet links, too!
www.bizrate.com- A great way to know you are dealing with a reputable compny, and they have links in every category.
www.amazon.com- I am thrilled you can finally order things for the home from Target…through Amazon.com.

Instructional

www.fauxlikeapro.com- Step by step faux finishing instruction.
www.dutchboy.com- Great info on all aspects of painting.
www.minwax.com- Ideas, projects, and instruction on wood finishing.
www.plaidonline.com- Many projects and products for decorative painting.
www.homedepot.com- Instruction for heavier projects like hanging blinds and wallpaper.

Don't overlook the frugal newsletters on the web though, they might be your best source for budget ideas! My suggestions?

www.stretcher.com
www.frugal-moms.com
www.frugalliving.about.com
www.frugalfamilynetwork.com
www.miserlymoms.com

I hope you have found this book to be informative and inspiring, and that you now have the confidence to make your house your "home", despite your budget limitations!

Notes

Notes

Notes

Kathleen Wilson

Kathleen Wilson

Kathleen Wilson

About The Author

Kathleen Wilson has worked in home and garden design since 1988. Mother of five kids and three stepchildren, she knows what she's talking about when it comes to tight budgets! Ms. Wilson shares her expert advice on her popular website and newsletter *The Budget Decorator,* which is available online at www.TheBudgetDecorator.com.

Printed in the United States
1021900004B/300